RENAISSANCE AND MODERN

renaissance and modern

Essays in Honor of Edwin M. Moseley

Edited by MURRAY J. LEVITH

SKIDMORE COLLEGE

1976

Copyright © 1976 by Skidmore College,
Saratoga Springs, New York 12866
Produced and distributed by Syracuse University Press,
Syracuse, New York 13210

First Edition

Library of Congress Cataloging in Publication Data

Main entry under title:

Renaissance and modern.

  Includes bibliographical references.
  CONTENTS: Hallam, G.   In praise of being a gentlemen.
—Cushner, A. W.   Some observations on Marlowe's
Edward II.—Levith, M. J.   Juliet's question and
Shakespeare's names.   [etc.]
    1.   English literature—History and criticism—
Addresses, essays, lectures.   2.   American literature—
History and criticism—Addresses, essays, lectures.
I.   Moseley, Edwin M., 1917–   II.   Levith, Murray J.
PR14.R43   820'.9   76–227
ISBN 0-8156-2177-9

Manufactured in the United States of America

Contents

MODERN

Edwin M. Moseley

EDWIN M. MOSELEY himself exhibited a few of those "significant gestures" he told us were characteristic of American writers of the '20s and '30s. He would enter class, place his folder of notes on the lectern, unbutton the pocket watch from his lapel (we wore "church keys" dangling from a string in imitation), and take attendance. The South Carolina dialect rolled out—to us as cultured, worldly, and exotic as any from Oxford in England. During the lecture itself, he sallied back and forth in front of us, explaining, asking, analyzing, provoking. He punctuated insights by smoothing his tie, lightly clapping his hands together, adjusting his jacket (he dressed immaculately), and doing what we called "deep knee bends." Like a pious man at prayer, he invoked the Muse of Learning with his wise and knowing incantations. Everything—absolutely everything—was written on the blackboard; significant words were connected with magical arrows, lines bisected circles, x's and y's were meaningfully juxtaposed. At the end of the class hour, when the writing and diagraming was complete and the blackboard was filled to the edges (as was his coat with chalk dust), Dr. Moseley would, with open hand, slap the board and declare: "It's all here! It's all here!" "It's all here," he would say again. It was for us, to be sure.

Professor Moseley's tenure at Washington and Jefferson College was just over a decade. During this time, that so small a school—well under a thousand—and one known primarily for its pre-medical program, should have turned out the number of eventual English Ph.D.s is remarkable. For every year that Dr. Moseley taught at Washington and Jefferson College, there is now at least one realized Ph.D. in English. But his appeal was not only for the literarily inclined. The pre-meds, dents, laws, and others flocked to his classes, were inspired by his lectures, and continue to acknowledge their debt to him. Dr. Henry Wechsler, Director of Research of the Medical Foundation of Boston, notes in a letter his "fond memories of Professor Moseley." Dr. Charles W. Lemmon, of the Mathematics Department at Queens College, remembers Dr. Moseley's teaching as "positively top-notch." Neurosurgeon Dr. Joel L. Falik, who also did graduate work in English, writes: "I feel that Dr. Moseley had a great influence as a teacher in the molding of my attitudes and character." Mr. Anthony P. Athens, Director of Financial Aid for the Community College of Allegheny County, Pennsylvania, writes simply that Dr. Moseley was "one of the finest men and undoubtedly the finest teacher I have ever known."

Some of us tried to emulate Professor Moseley quite precisely. Since he received a Ph.D. and was teaching literature on the college level, we wanted to do the same. A number of us even went to "his" graduate school, Syracuse University. After he left Washington and Jefferson to become Dean of the Faculty and Professor of English at Skidmore College, we formed a sort of informal club at Syracuse and each summer would travel (often with his students from other graduate schools throughout the country) to Saratoga Springs, New York, to refresh ourselves with the Moseley waters. During these visits, he invariably lightened the weight of our previous graduate school year with words of encouragement. We had lively literary discussions on such occasions, were brought up to date on the activities of our classmates, and would tell and retell old stories. One such was how our award-winning literary magazine, advised by Dr. Moseley, received its name. Following the second world war a number of returned veterans appeared in Professor Moseley's creative writing class. Among the readings for the course were two stories titled "The Wall," one by Jean-Paul Sartre and the other by John Hersey. As a joke on their professor, for a weekly assignment all of the students in the class wrote pieces with the same title, "The Wall." When the college literary magazine was started by members of this class shortly thereafter, it obviously had to be called *The Wall*.

We learned much from him about teaching by remembering his methods. His style was Socratic and genteel. He forgave ignorance and naiveté, and made each student feel bright and unique. One was *never* wrong in class. Somehow the most illogical, ill-conceived, off-base comment or opinion would be shaped and molded by him into something contributory. No one felt uncomfortable in his classes. Imaginations flourished.

His range of allusion—the "frame of reference" he was always trying to broaden in us—was far-ranging indeed. Professor William Rankin, from the University of Zaire in Africa, remembers that "Dr. Moseley always used to amaze his students, and even frighten us, by his capacity to recognize similarities in the most disparate things— Renaissance literature, Modern literature, exotic paintings, good and even impossibly bad movies, as well as life situations." As freshmen, many of us received our first art history lessons from Professor Moseley, our first instruction in philosophy and psychology, our first political theory. We learned to handle terms like "existentialism," "archetypal," "Marxian dialectic." The books he cited sounded so interesting when he spoke of them that we wanted to read them ourselves.

His comments on papers were always critically helpful but gentle. He was generous and encouraging. I once asked if a paper I had written on Katherine Anne Porter's "Old Mortality" was publishable. Some excerpts from his answer follow:

Your paper is all that I have said—in terms of what I asked you to do. For an article to be published, however . . . .
Too, I haven't read *Understanding Fiction* on "Old Mortality" for a long time, but I wonder if, . . . though you have some ideas they [Brooks and Warren] do not touch on, and have stated in your own way—which make them yours.
What I say here does not belittle your paper in the least.
I suggest that you read some articles in, say . . . .
I give you this copy of *College English* not because my item on Edith Wharton is an ideal piece of criticism, but . . . .

Edwin M. Moseley received his undergraduate degree *summa cum laude* from the College of Charleston in South Carolina. His M.A. and Ph.D. are from Syracuse University, where he taught as a graduate assistant. After one year as Assistant Professor at Evansville College in Indiana, he came to Washington and Jefferson College where he taught from 1948 to 1961, moving up through the professorial ranks. He left to become Dean of the Faculty and Professor of English at Skidmore College. He is currently Provost, Dean of the Faculty, and Professor of English at Skidmore.

In addition to a distinguished teaching career, he has lectured and published widely, especially in the fields of Renaissance and Modern literature. With Robert Ashley, he edited the *Elizabethan Fiction* volume in the Rinehart series which is still in print after more than twenty years. A monograph, *F. Scott Fitzgerald*, was published by Eerdmans for the "Contemporary Writers in Christian Perspective" series. And his book, *Pseudonyms of Christ in the Modern Novel*, published by the University of Pittsburgh Press in 1963, won praise from such noted critics as Milton R. Stern, Chad Walsh, and Stanley Edgar Hyman.

In the acknowledgments to *Pseudonyms of Christ in the Modern Novel*, Dr. Moseley thanks his "many . . . students who have contributed to it by listening to, discussing in, and writing for my classes . . . at Washington and Jefferson College." This volume, *Renaissance and Modern*, Dr. Moseley's fields of special interest, is our way of thanking *him* for those classes. To paraphrase what the great Renaissance teacher Roger Ascham said of Sir John Cheke, he was for many of us "teacher of all the little poore learning we have."

Saratoga Springs, N.Y.   Murray J. Levith
Spring 1976

Preface

THE TITLE of this volume of critical essays is meant to indicate the broad historical range of its content. Moreover, I have interpreted *Renaissance* to include everything from Castiglione to Marvell, and *Modern* to permit Jean Toomer, Katherine Mansfield, and Glenway Wescott.

The essays contained herein are as various in style and scope as they are in subject matter. We begin with George Hallam's reminders of the history and focal idea of Castiglione's most graceful of works, *The Courtier*—surely one of the seminal documents of the Renaissance. There follows Arnold Cushner's reading of some issues raised by Marlowe's *Edward II*, the muscular play about a homosexual king. My own essay attempts to organize Shakespearean nomenclature into useful categories, and to suggest that names in Shakespeare are often deliberate and a helpful tool for reading the plays. Roger Rollin provides us with a "modern" psychoanalytic reading of Milton's great poem, applying some of Norman N. Holland's techniques. Finally for the "Renaissance" section is a totally new and comprehensive explication of Marvell's *Upon Appleton House*. James Kiehl makes sense out of what until now has seemed hopelessly obscure in the poem.

If poets and playwrights are favored in the "Renaissance" part, some major writers of fiction receive attention among the "Moderns." Joseph Conrad's Russian novel, *Under Western Eyes*, is the subject of Donald Swanson's piece. He is interested in its unusual point of view.

Sanford Pinsker's essay notices the various kinds of "ghosts" that haunt Joyce's *Ulysses*. Works by William Faulkner and Ernest Hemingway are subjects for the next chapters. Lee Richmond argues for the complexity and importance of the character Vardaman Bundren in Faulkner's *As I Lay Dying*. Joseph DeFalco treats the political works of Hemingway's "middle period." Two apparently dissimilar writers, Jean Toomer and Katherine Mansfield, share a mystical groping after the ineffable—so claims William Rankin. And we end with Glenway Wescott, a contemporary who has not received his share of attention. Alfred Kolb affords us a close look at Wescott's first novel, *The Apple of the Eye*.

MJL

Acknowledgments

President Joseph C. Palamountain and the Board of Trustees of Skidmore College deserve special thanks for help with this project. Richard C. Stephens, Director of Alumni Activities for Washington and Jefferson College, helped locate potential contributors. Ralph Ciancio helped in an editorial way, Jim Kiehl in many ways. Kathy Palmer typed. Carol Goldberg typed even more and up to the last minute. James Kettlewell, Curator of the Hyde Collection, Glens Falls, New York, allowed the illustrations. And, to be sure, the most thanks to Tina, who is as charmed by Edwin as we all were by Dr. Moseley.

MJL

Contributors

George Hallam is Professor of English at Jacksonville University, where he has taught since 1957. His graduate degrees are from the University of Florida. He is both a scholar and teacher of the English Renaissance. Among his publications is an essay on *"sprezzatura"* which appeared in the *Southern Humanities Review*.

Arnold W. Cushner's M.A. is from the State University of New York at Buffalo and his Ph.D. is from Case Western Reserve University. He has taught at Franklin and Marshall College and at Allegheny College. As he puts it, "the current job market has driven me into government work"; he is employed now by the Pennsylvania Department of Justice in the Bureau of Consumer Protection.

Murray J. Levith has an M.A. from the University of Nebraska and a Ph.D. from Syracuse University. He is Assistant Professor of English at Skidmore College and is currently working on a full-length study of names in Shakespeare.

Roger B. Rollin is William James Lemon Professor of Literature at Clemson University. He has published widely on the seventeenth century, and his book on Robert Herrick is highly regarded. He is an avid student of popular culture. An anthology he edited, *Hero/Anti-Hero*, was published recently. His graduate degrees are from Yale University.

James M. Kiehl received the Ph.D. from Syracuse University and is Assistant Professor at Skidmore College. His publications include a recent essay on the poetry of Howard Nemerov and a commentary on artist Richard Upton's series of prints on Milton's *Paradise Lost*. He has a special interest in film.

Donald R. Swanson is Professor of English at Wright State University. He is a member of the Board of Directors of the College English Association and Chairman of its Publication Committee. He has published numerous articles on nineteenth and twentieth century British and American authors, and has written a book on George Meredith. Another book, on the English novelist Richard Hughes, is in press. His M.A. is from the University of Connecticut and his Ph.D. is from Rutgers University.

Sanford Pinsker holds graduate degrees from the University of Washington and is Associate Professor at Franklin and Marshall College. A prolific poet and critic, he has published extensively. *The Schlemiel as Metaphor* appeared in 1971 and *Still Life and Other Poems* in 1975. Two books, one on Joseph Conrad and the other on Philip Roth, are forthcoming.

Lee J. Richmond teaches at St. John's University, and his graduate degrees are from Syracuse University. At present he is working on a study of Thomas Pynchon.

Joseph M. DeFalco is Professor of English at Marquette University. His M.A. and Ph.D. were earned at the University of Florida. His *The Hero in Hemingway's Short Stories* is the only book-length study of its subject. Recent articles on Hemingway have appeared in *Hemingway in Our Time* and the *Lost Generation Journal*. In 1971 he edited the Collected Poems of Christopher Pearse Cranch. He is a member of the bibliography committee of *Twentieth Century Literature.*

William Rankin did graduate work at Brown University, the University of Madras in India, the School of Living Oriental Languages in Paris, and the University of Oregon, where he received his Ph.D. He teaches English literature at the University of Zaire in Lubumbashi.

Alfred Kolb is Associate Professor of English and Head of the Department of English, Foreign Languages, and Music at Mercer County Community College. He also teaches German and is especially interested in the relationships between German and American literature. His work on Friedrich Gerstäcker has been published in several places. His graduate degrees are from Syracuse University.

RENAISSANCE AND MODERN

Renaissance

Raphael, "Portrait of a Young Man," ca. 1510.
Courtesy of the Hyde Collection, Glens Falls, New York

1

In Praise of Being a Gentleman: 1528-1976

George Hallam

Among rare books Castiglione's *The Courtier* must be a feather-weight. The 1528 Firenze edition in the University of Florida library, for instance, weighs exactly eleven ounces. Not even a pound. Hardly more than a plume. In fact, sitting at the polished Queen Anne table and hefting the small book once or twice, one has the strange sensation that here is nothing at all—the aged calf binding and the heavy dark print notwithstanding. In a word, Castiglione's polite fiction is contemporary enough to be weightless.

But of course Castiglione is not our contemporary. True, the latest *Books in Print* lists four editions, and the popular Anchor translation of 1959 by Charles S. Singleton continues to show among the paperbacks. Yet who dares doubt that in an age when noble spirits and modest souls have little appeal, the days are numbered for Castiglione's charm piece. That impertinent juxta-position a few years back (in a glossy text called *Two Ways of Seeing*[1]) of one of Sidney's sonnets to Stella and a black-and-white photograph of a motorcyclist and his girlfriend astride a surly Harley-Davidson was surely a measure of insults to come.

In the meantime, *The Courtier* will remain a rare book, a

---

1. Wilson G. Pinney, ed. (Boston: Little, Brown, 1971), pp. 136–137.

featherweight of refined talk and jolly haggling over something called *virtú*. If nothing else, for the curious reader the book will stand as a quaint reminder of a concern that supposedly cut deep into manners during Shakespeare's day—courtesy, that is, whether false or real. For others, there may at least be room for it in their own private bag of literary delights. Something to pull out occasionally for instant amusement. Perhaps the title alone will then suffice: *Il Cortegiano . . . Il Cortegiano.*

For the literary sentimentalist, *The Courtier* will of course do more. It will recall the simple, pleasant fact that more than four hundred years ago there lived in Mantua a gentle count who, apparently with some misgivings, wrote a longish civilized book which, even were it dismissed tomorrow as an anachronism, has had its say—having etched out a remarkable history of publication, attracted a fair amount of critical attention, bred its own delicate balance concerning ideal human posture, and charmed four centuries of readers into believing that the social graces *will* have everlasting life on earth.

The basic facts of *The Courtier's* composition and first publication are satisfying to recall. An outgrowth of that seamless climate of good taste and refinement at Urbino, *The Courtier* apparently took form in 1508, slipped into limited private circulation by 1516, then encountered much delay and revision (the last in Spain) during the next twelve years until Castiglione felt compelled to authorize the first edition in Venice in 1528, a year before he died. What followed is fairly common knowledge: by the end of the century, Italian presses had printed forty-nine editions (some authorities say fifty), and the work had appeared in French, Spanish, Latin, and English translations.[2]

In the sixteenth century, this publishing triumph was marred only by the book's falling into disfavor with the Inquisition in 1576 and the Index in 1590. Subsequent centuries were to make less fuss over courtesy and chivalry, and to write less in praise of being a gentleman. Yet they were to be kind to *The Courtier* in

2. C. P. Merlino, "A Valuable Collection of Castiglione's *Cortegiano*," *Italica* 9 (June 1932):38. The acquisition in 1932 by the University of Michigan of thirty-nine editions of *The Courtier*—all but five of them sixteenth century copies, and one "a beautiful Aldine"—is a delightful reminder of Castiglione's early fame.

their fashion. If we are to trust a statement made in 1959 by Julius A. Molinaro that "since April, 1528, . . . more than 176 editions of this Renaissance classic have appeared in several European languages,"[3] the present total figure of nearly 180, by rough count, is astonishing.

Just as it is tempting while sitting quietly in a rare book room to consider the twenty years Castiglione spent composing *The Courtier* as a grand gesture of *sprezzatura*, so it is equally tempting to imagine that when he finally presented the sickly Pope Clement VII with a privately printed copy of the book in Orvieto in 1528, he knew perfectly well he had fashioned a masterpiece. Yet it would be foolish to suppose in turn that during the last days of his life as Bishop of Avila, Castiglione had any notion that his charming dialogue would become anything more than useful diversion—that it would acquire immense fame and become an object for scholarly discussion and debate.

Both the Laurentian manuscript at Florence, still the standard text for editors and translators, and the original English version by Sir Thomas Hoby remain of greatest historical interest for the general scholar. Until at least 1900, as Walter Raleigh noted in the Tudor Translations reprint, Hoby's version had held its own among other English renditions.[4] Even Professor Molinaro, in the *Italica* article mentioned above, after reminding us via F. O. Matthiessen of Hoby's serious deficiencies as a translator, grudgingly acknowledges his colorful and forceful language.[5]

Hoby's translation arrived in 1561, ten years before a popular Latin version by Bartholomew Clerke and well in time to win praise from Roger Ascham and John Florio and to influence Marlowe, Sidney, Spenser, Shakespeare, Jonson, Harvey, and undoubtedly many others. Not only did it introduce the concept of *sprezzatura* to English writers, but it was popular enough in other respects to deserve reprints in 1577, 1588, and 1603.

However, the book received some curious editing along the

---

3. "Castiglione and His English Translators," *Italica* 36 (December 1959):262.
4. *The Book of The Courtier* (New York: AMS Press, 1967). See Raleigh's introduction, lix–lxi.
5. Matthiessen's charges are in his *Translation: An Elizabethan Art* (Cambridge, Mass.: Harvard University Press, 1931), p. 22.

way. In the 1588 trilingual reprint one John Wolfe, whom John
L. Lievsay cites as "the most important printer of Italian books
in London" between 1579 and 1601, seems to have altered Hoby
at will.[6] Take, for example, the very word *sprezzatura:* "to use in
euery thyng a certaine Recklessness, to couer arte withall" in
Hoby, becomes "to use in euerye thing a certaine disgracing to
couer arte withall" in Wolfe.

Hoby had used *disgracing* (as well as *dispraysing* and *curi-
ousness*) elsewhere in his text, but he preferred *recklessness.* As
editors Lamson and Smith noted some years ago, Hoby's *recklessness* was an unfortunate rendition of the Italian.[7] But what could
be more unfortunate than printer Wolfe's silent emendation along
with the questionable connotation attached to a word like
disgracing?

This is a small matter, perhaps not worth mentioning, except
one discovers that the Everyman series chose for its text the 1588
reprint rather than the 1561 original.[8] Over the years *sprezzatura*
has been variously rendered: *negligence, careless ease, easy grace,
studied carelessness,* and *nonchalance* to mention a few. Of these,
either *studied carelessness* or *nonchalance* seems most fitting,
preferably the latter. *Sprezzatura* in this sense has anchored the
popular Singleton translation for fifteen years,[9] and also appears
alongside *studied carelessness* in the 1968 Follett/Zanichelli
Italian Dictionary (also in Gabriel Chapuis' French column in
Wolfe's polyglot reprint of 1588).

The matter is also worth mentioning because *sprezzatura* is
Castiglione's *idée fixe.* The bibliography of articles and books on
Castiglione ranges over a variety of topics, from the dialectic of
The Courtier to its author's place on the Renaissance ladder of
love and his influence on William Butler Yeats. But probably no
topic has proved more attractive or aroused more general interest
than *sprezzatura.* One thinks immediately of the chapter in Ken-
neth O. Myrick's *Sir Philip Sidney as a Literary Craftsman.*[10] If

6. *The Englishman's Italian Books, 1500–1700* (Philadelphia, Pa.: University of
Pennsylvania Press, 1969), p. 16.
7. In *The Golden Hind* (New York: Norton, 1956), p. 116.
8. *The Book of The Courtier* (New York: Dutton, 1948). See introduction, x.
9. Charles S. Singleton, trans., *The Book of The Courtier* (Garden City: Doubleday, 1959), p. 43.
10. (Cambridge, Mass.: Harvard University Press, 1935). See the final chapter.

references to *sprezzatura* since then have been scattered and general, it is probably because Myrick left little to be said. When one thinks of Castiglione, one thinks of *sprezzatura*, not of Platonic love or how to mount a horse.

The first three books of *The Courtier* are supposed to be indebted to Aristotle's *Nicomachean Ethics*.[11] Blended in with these virtues is Castiglione's emphasis upon grace and *sprezzatura*, with *sprezzatura* the essential—essential because it is the outward manner of expressing the inward virtue. But Castiglione wanted *sprezzatura* to seem—rather, be—the virtue, too, and whether that is possible or not is a good question.

If Hoby's use of *recklessness* misled his contemporaries away from Castiglione's intention of a *natural*, easy grace to something contrived, this was probably of little moment. Given their attraction to bravery, the Elizabethans really did not want to "eschew Affection." Anything cultivated or designed or imitated suited them well enough, whether or not the manner be called *sprezzatura*.

But today emotional responses outweigh grace notes. Four and a half centuries have done much to deflate the aristocratic temper *sprezzatura* was tailored for. Though it has been kept alive, often informally, by those concerned with equanimity, with the fitness of things, and with the ability to carry one's attainments lightly, its place among today's lifestyles is suspect.

A little rhetoric can be impressive. Consider this short specimen from the author's essay on "*Sprezzatura*—For the Man Who Has Everything":

The word comes from Italian *sprezzare* (to despise, distain, scorn), and . . . implies a contempt for the notion that you must prove your good breeding. Thus construed, *sprezzatura* turns the mind from outer to inner qualities and values. If you find the moderate and the disciplined more to your liking than the boorish and the promiscuous; if you prefer discrimination and taste to vulgarity and crassness; if you favor the silent commitment over self-advertisement; if you think modesty a virtue and immodesty a vice;

---

11. See Albert D. Menut, "Castiglione and the Nicomachean Ethics," *PMLA* 57 (1943):309–21.

if you believe well-doing is superior to well-knowing—then *sprez-zatura* is your patron.[12]

There was a business executive taken enough with these words to quote them once in a speech. Several years later, however, he decided on a change in his lifestyle. He decided to show "a little something around the edges," to project an honest look. So he grew a beard, shed his business-executive look, and became a connoisseur of the arts. By now he had second thoughts about *sprezzatura*—even though his "studied carelessness" had indeed moved him closer to it—and suspected something spurious about the concept. He was correct. *Sprezzatura* is basically a pose.

No one knew this better than Castiglione himself. No sooner had he finished his dialogue on the lighter expressions of art and behavior in 1516 than he became bored with it. Ralph Roeder suggests why:

> For in that year something had occurred, something which had long been maturing and which now came to light. He had out-grown his past. The life of the Courtier was a phantom existence, not only because, as he now realized, it was a pose. All its aims— culture, ideals, friendship—were mere semblances of life, refined illusions of reality, eclipsed at last by a genuine experience. For the first time, a profound and uncultivated feeling possessed him; and beside it the conventional sentiments of his youth paled into insignificance. The self-sufficiency of virtue, the disinterested pur-suit of honor, the fugitive pleasures of society, the half-measures of friendship, now appeared no more than green conceits, fond infatuations, and the book based on them a literary exercise with-out vital meaning. He was passionately in love with his wife.[13]

Castiglione had entered into a marriage produced by one of his mother's constant matchmakings and at a time when he had stood vulnerable to life's "physical offenses."

12. *Southern Humanities Review* 3 (Spring 1969):177.
13. *The Man of the Renaissance* (New York: Time, 1966), p. 366.

But life and love do not last. In 1519, after three years of good marriage, Ippolita Torelli died in childbirth, and Castiglione considered his future: should he continue with experience in a changing world led now by the vulgarities of an Aretino, or revert to the memories of the Court of Urbino, retreat into his fantasy of manners (what Roeder somewhat cruelly, if brilliantly, calls being "once more the impersonal spectator of his own existence")? Castiglione chose the fantasy of manners.

But not without a struggle. The twelve years before *The Courtier* was published consisted in trying to resolve the problem of how the individual who is a social being can be accountable to himself as well as to others. The answer lay in *sprezzatura*.

Even though *sprezzatura* is basically a pose, Castiglione hoped that with it a man could so steel himself in self-discipline that the cultivated would appear natural, would in effect *become* natural. That this was his intention is seen in a thorough study published by Dr. Walter Schrinner in Berlin in 1939, *Castiglione und die Englische Renaissance.*[14] Dr. Schrinner saw the uniqueness of Castiglione's concept: how it aimed not to pose or affect but to develop an absolute control over one's true inner feelings— a goal for the chosen few, the highest form of discipline, without arrogance and with full knowledge of the quality of character involved.

The other half of Castiglione's struggle moved outwardly toward a staunch give and take. The individual as a social being must make a gesture of compromise—that is, compromise of a high order, perhaps best seen in a shrewd observation by Hugh Kenner. Speaking in another context, Kenner envisions the virtues of detachment and involvement nicely balanced: "one does not ever know securely which side to take, all sides excluding what wants to be conserved; but one holds, being civilized, all urgencies in balance, and makes, from time to time, pragmatic commitments; . . . one's final commitment is to . . . civilization. Civilization fused with local urgency is at its rare best the formula for

14. The date raises interesting questions, but one remembers the striking statement in Book I of *The Courtier:* "I am of the opinion that the principal and true profession of the courtier ought to be that of arms."

poise."[15] What else is at the heart of *sprezzatura* than a well-bred poise, whether one's birth is noble or humble?

Seen thus in terms of Castiglione's struggle, *sprezzatura* bridges the gap between the experience itself and living it—yet somehow being the experience, too. It is debatable whether or not Castiglione succeeded in ironing out the intricacies of this paradox. But the verdict here is to accept the marvelous apotheosis Roeder describes:

> After believing in everything and everyone else, Castiglione was at last forced in self-defence to believe in himself; and he withdrew in a moral recessional through ever older and older selves to his first fundamental faith. *The Courtier* contained it; he had carried it through life; and the hesitations and delays which had retarded its appearance seemed to have reserved it for the moment when it was most needed. For the hour was supremely apt. After a cataclysm which had swept away the basic sanctities and the commonest decencies of civilized life, it was time for a gesture of moral luxury, time to declare his faith in the amenities of life, because of their very futility. The hour of abysmal brutality was the hour to repeat that what mattered in life was not its object but the manner of living it. And *The Courtier*, so long in maturing and so often remoulded, underwent one more transformation in his mind and emerged with a new value and its last moral meaning. It was his religion.[16]

Castiglione's ostensible reason for authorizing an edition of *The Courtier* in 1528 was to forestall an unauthorized edition set in motion by a female admirer Vittoria Collona. A more pleasant thought is that he would have agreed to publication anyhow, because he had finally accepted the way of life embodied in the book.

15. A note on Andrew Marvell, in *Seventeenth Century Poetry* (New York: Holt, Rinehart, and Winston, 1964), p. 444.
16. *Man of the Renaissance,* p. 451.

Some Observations on Marlowe's *Edward II*

Arnold W. Cushner

MARLOWE'S *Edward II* is an intriguing play with impact for the most critical of readers. Yet, its themes are largely inconsistent, its characterizations are often incredible, and its verse is mostly indifferent. In short, the impact left by the whole is far greater than the sum of the parts. The question, of course, is why should this be, and the answer lies in the continued pertinence of Marlowe's concerns in the play. These concerns—involving personal relationships, social institutions, and change—are the subjects of the following observations.

Marlowe's portrayal of the characters of the homosexual king Edward, his "minion" Gaveston, the Young Mortimer, and their interaction, is central to the drama. In the play's initial speech, Marlowe depicts Gaveston's single-minded obsession with his "sweet prince"

> (whose) amorous lines
> Might have enforc'd me to have swum from France
> And, like Leander, gasp'd upon the sand
> So thou would'st smile and take me in thine arms!
> The sight of London to my exil'd eyes
> Is as Elysium to a new-come soul.
> —Not that I love the city or the men
> But that it harbors him I hold so dear

> The King—upon whose bosom let me die
> And with the world be still at enmity!
>
> (I.i.6–15)[1]

This speech—with its inflated, romantic diction and myth-ological allusions—displays the elements of Gaveston's shaping of reality. The expression of his feelings for Edward in the hyper-bolic language of the sonnet is the verbal manifestation of his obsessive love. Given the exalted intensity of this love, it is no wonder Gaveston is unaffected by the disruption it causes the realm. Politics and order are mere sublunar concerns.

Yet such is to describe Gaveston in a way that makes him appear far more self-conscious of his language and behavior than he actually is. His rhetoric and mythologizing are the natural out-pourings of his sensibility. He is not devious or simply malicious when he perfunctorily dismisses the three "Poor Men" in the first scene; his reaction, rather, is a function of his nature:

> These are not men for me.
> I must have wanton poets, pleasant wits,
> Musicians that with touching of a string
> May draw the pliant King which way I please.
>
> (I.i.50–53)

His nature is that of the esthete: of "Sweet speeches, comedies, and pleasing shows" (I.i.56).

Such a sensibility, even if it inclined Gaveston toward in-nocent behavior, which it does not, would inevitably cause a clash with the warriors, politicians, and churchmen in the society. A clash has occurred before the play begins (leading to Gaveston's original exile) and is the central action of the play itself. Chief among those who oppose Gaveston is the Young Mortimer, al-though it is his uncle who sets the opposition when he tells Ed-ward: "If you love us, my lord, hate Gaveston" (I.i.80). The

1. Leo Kirschbaum, ed., *The Plays of Christopher Marlowe* (Cleveland, Ohio: World, 1962). Subsequent references are to this edition and are given parenthet-ically in the text.

specifics of the complaint the nobles have against Gaveston are more implicit than explicit. He is called "base and obscure" by Lancaster, but a resentment of these qualities hardly seems to justify the unveiled threats of revolt made to the King if he does not exile Gaveston. Some explanation for "base and obscure" is found at the end of the act, though, when Young Mortimer asserts:

> But this I scorn, that one so basely born
> Should by his sovereign's favour grow so pert
> And riot it with the treasure of the realm
> While soldiers mutiny, for want of pay—.
> He wears a lord's revenue on his back,
> And Midas-like he jets it in the court
> With base outlandish cullions at his heels
> Whose proud fantastic liveries make such show
> As if that Proteus, god of shapes, appear'd!
> (I.iv.405–13)

The nobles are concerned with the court's transformation into a place of "sweet speeches, comedies, and pleasing shows." The nobles follow a life of arms and of combat, epitomized by the Young Mortimer.

Mortimer is cast from the same mold as Shakespeare's Hotspur; he is impetuous, quick-tempered, and militant. But there is no scene that gives Mortimer the depth that we find in, for instance, Hotspur's scene with his wife. Mortimer's outburst after being urged by Warwick to restrain himself is typical:

> I cannot, nor I will not. I must speak.
> Cousin, our hands I hope shall fence our heads
> And strike off his that makes you threaten us.
> Come, uncle, let us leave the brain-sick King
> And henceforth parle with our naked swords.
> (I.i.122–26)

Whenever Mortimer speaks, his words and images suggest action: "We'll hale him [Gaveston] from the bosom of the King /

And at the court-gate hang the peasant up" (I.ii.20–30); "Curse him [Edward], if he refuse [to allow Gaveston's exile]; and then may we / Depose him and elect another king" (I.iv.54–55); or "But whiles I have a sword, a hand, a heart, / I will not yield to any such upstart [Gaveston]" (I.iv.422–23).

The third character, the King, is more complex than either Gaveston or Mortimer. His character is shaped by the narrow hedonistic desires of the moment; what makes Marlowe's portrayal of him masterful is that Edward sustains our interest even as he is largely reprehensible morally and incompetent politically. Edward's obdurate defense to the nobles of his right to recall Gaveston, as well as his immediate response to Gaveston's return ("What, Gaveston! Welcome! Kiss not my hand— / Embrace me, Gaveston, as I do thee" [I.i.139–40]), leaves no doubt as to his allegiance.

Much has been written about Marlowe's own sexual predilection; his reputed statement, "that all they that love not Tobacco & Boies were fools," is inevitably quoted. But clearly the portrayal of homosexual love in this play is anything but sympathetic or apologetic. The Edward-Gaveston relationship (and later the Edward-Spenser relationship) is destructive on all levels—politically, familially, personally. The ennobling effects of male relationships—reasonableness, fidelity, temperance, qualities argued for in, for instance, Shakespeare's sonnets—are absent from this play. Nor can it be argued that Marlowe was only being faithful to his source; for as Michel Poirier points out, "Marlowe insistently stresses what Holinshed mentioned discreetly in his Chronicle."[2] If anything, the homosexual relationship portrayed in the play would seem to set Renaissance Gay Liberation back a step or two.

Marlowe's portrayal of the King and his relationship with Gaveston makes sense if viewed as the last degenerative gasps of the medieval courtly love tradition, stripped of all its conventions, refinements, and subtleties. All that remains of the tradition in this play is an obsessive passion—a passion that lacks any of the redeeming or ennobling qualities of courtly love's earlier, heterosexual conventions. Satisfying the passion has come to be the ex-

2. *Christopher Marlowe* (Hamden, Conn.: Archon, 1968), p. 38.

clusive goal of the relationship; there are neither secret, selfless deeds performed in the name of love, nor stolen moments of secret intimacy. Nothing about this relationship is secret. One has no reason to doubt Isabella's description of the King and Gaveston as she laments her own fate to Young Mortimer:

> For now my lord the King regards me not,
> But dotes upon the love of Gaveston—
> He clasps his cheeks, and hangs about his neck,
> Smiles in his face, and whispers in his ears—
> And when I come he frowns, as who should say,
> "Go whither thou wilt seeing I have Gaveston!"
>   (I.ii.49–54)

Yet this relationship in part gives the play its impact and dramatic interest because the decadent Edward-Gaveston relationship becomes a metaphor for the larger decadence of the social order and institutions. The play presents a world of fragmented values and lost ideals. Not only has the code of courtly love reached an irretrievably degenerate point, but religious and political values have come to a similar end. These have been replaced by liberalizing religious forces and democratizing political ones. To put it another way, the play reflects the shift from medieval idealism to Renaissance pragmatism. As the Young Spenser has it: "You must be proud, bold, pleasant, resolute: / And now and then stab as occasion serves" (II.i.42–43).

The Church no longer serves as a force that can stimulate moral behavior and, in fact, can only compel obedience through threat. It is after the Archbishop of Canterbury threatens to "discharge these lords / Of duty and allegiance due to thee" (I.iv. 61–62) that the King agrees to exile Gaveston.

Moreover, although Edward's consequent outcry against the archbishop had its obvious appeal to Marlowe's English Reformation audience, it exudes a viciousness that is as anti-religious as it is anti-papist.

> Why should a king be subject to a priest?
> Proud Rome, that hatchest such imperial grooms,

> For these thy superstitious taper-lights,
> Wherewith thy antichristian churches blaze,
> I'll fire thy crazed buildings and enforce
> The papal towers to kiss the lowly ground!
> (I.iv.97–102)

Such savagery is used, of course, to portray Edward unfavorably. But beyond that, only in an atmosphere where the Church's influence has seriously deteriorated can a threat such as this, even though it is in soliloquy, be uttered.

In the realm of politics and with the relationship between the King and Young Mortimer, however, the shift between the old, lost idealism and the new pragmatism can be seen most clearly. Commentaries on Shakespeare's *Richard II* speak of the poetic or dramatic Richard being supplanted by the efficient, bureaucratic Bolingbroke. This sort of displacement occurs even more obviously in *Edward II*.

Marlowe knows as well as Shakespeare the orthodoxy of Tudor absolutism. Yet in this play Marlowe gives it nothing more than lip service. Where the divine right of kings is asserted, it seems desirable to see it honored in the breach rather than in the observance.

After Isabella's description of Edward's behavior with Gaveston quoted earlier, Young Mortimer asserts that the

> sly inveigling Frenchman we'll exile,
> or lose our lives. And yet, ere that day come,
> The king shall lose his crown, for we have power,
> And courage too, to be reveng'd at full.
> (I.ii.57–60)

This suggestion of deposition immediately brings responses consistent with Tudor orthodoxy:

A. of Cant. But yet lift not your swords against
          the king.
Lanc.   No but we'll lift Gaveston from hence.

War.   And war must be the means, or he'll stay still.
Isab.   Then let him stay. For rather than my lord
            Shall be oppress'd by civil mutinies,
            I will endure a melancholy life.
            —And let him frolic with his minion.

                                                (I.ii.61–67)

Even this early in the play we have had ample evidence of Edward's unfitness to rule, an unfitness no doubt apparent even to the most conservative member of Marlowe's audience and on stage exceeding that of Shakespeare's Richard II.

But beyond Edward's unfitness to rule, Marlowe seems to be at best indifferent to the providential view of history and at worst a prognosticator of its passing. As the nobles are about to storm the walls of Tynemouth Castle in open rebellion against the King, for instance, Marlowe has Lancaster say almost incidentally, "None be so hardy as to touch the King" (I.iv.28). The letter of absolutism is acknowledged, but its spirit is certainly lost. In its place, Marlowe at least hints at an inchoate democracy, articulated by Mortimer and supported by the commons.

Mortimer continually asserts legal justifications for deposition. He argues that if the King fails to exile Gaveston against the will of the nobles, "Then may we lawfully revolt from him" (I.ii.73). Later when the King is recalcitrant in signing the document exiling Gaveston, Mortimer says, "Curse him, if he refuse; and then may we / Depose him and elect another king!" (I.iv.54–55).

Such statements suggest a shift in thinking away from the old declining autocracy toward the new incipient democracy. The issue is momentarily emphasized in Act III, scene ii when, as the nobles are about to do battle with the forces of the King, Warwick asserts, "Alarum to fight! St. George for England, and the barons' right!" (221–22). To which Edward rejoins: "St. George for England, and King Edward's right" (223).

It is in the final two acts, though, with the direct confrontations between Edward and Mortimer, that the play between old and new comes to the surface. The supporting characters are gone—Lancaster, Warwick, Pembroke for Mortimer; Gaveston for Edward. The new allies (Hainault and Young Spencer) are cardboard imitations of their predecessors. And the new order represented by Mortimer, at least temporarily, carries the day. It is a prudent and practical Mortimer, if not a sincere one, who answers Kent's question about the fate of Edward with, "'Tis not in her [the Queen's] controlment, nor in ours, / But as the realm and parliament shall please" (IV.v.44–45). The fate of Edward at this point is sealed regardless of who finally decides; nevertheless, there is a deference to something other than autocratic will.

The unresolved question of the play is where Marlowe stands in all of this. He does not attempt to justify the whimpish King who wants only "some nook or corner . . . / To frolic with my dearest Gaveston" (I.iv.72–73). Yet, in the last two acts the King, if not a better person, at least elicits some sympathy. On the other hand, Mortimer, whose earlier rightness of purpose made his actions admirable becomes repugnant in the last two acts. Certainly the King's earlier autocratic ways were no worse than Mortimer's Machiavellianism:

> The Prince I rule, the Queen do I command,
> And with a lowly congé to the ground,
> The proudest lords salute me as I pass.
> I seal, I cancel, I do what I will.
> Fear'd am I more than lov'd—let me be fear'd
> And when I frown make all the court look pale.
> (V.iv.48–53)

Marlowe, it would appear, cannot make up his mind and gives us few hints as to how we are to respond. A kind of cynicism runs through the play, suggesting that nothing is worthwhile or has a good end.

I mentioned earlier the decadence of the old order, epitomized by the perverse, consuming love of the King and Gaveston, being challenged and overcome by the new order in the person of the vigorous, somewhat impetuous Mortimer. What the new order has to offer, however—and this seems the reason Marlowe concentrates on the King's torture and death scene so—is the sadism of Matrevis, Gurney, and Lightborn. Calculated Machiavellianism and restrained, efficient violence replace homosexual obsession. Which, Marlowe seems to ask, do we want?

He gives us only one other choice, a contrived one involving the young Prince. It is difficult to believe that Marlowe's audience was convinced that Edward III provides salvation for the world he now rules; it is difficult for a twentieth-century audience to accept, also. Although the new King's concluding words demonstrate proper and sincere filial piety, they never escape the conventional:

> Sweet father, here unto thy murder'd ghost
> I offer up this wicked traitor's head.
> And let these tears, distilling from mine eyes,
> Be witness to my grief and innocency.
> (V.vi.99–102)

The play has a surface moral progression from sin to innocence, from the declamations of the base Gaveston and the obsessed king to the elegies of the innocent, new-crowned prince. Under the surface, however, the play never establishes political or moral norms. Those noble values expressed in the play are ambiguous and occur when characters confront death. Even Marlowe's cynicism cannot fully contain the admirable durability of Edward in the dungeon:

> And there in mire and puddle have I stood
> This ten days' space, and lest that I should sleep,
> One plays continually upon a drum.
> They give me bread and water, being a king!
> So that for want of sleep and sustenance
> My mind's distemper'd, and my body's numb'd,
> And whether I have limbs or no I know not.
> O, would my blood dropp'd out from every vein
> As doth this water from my tatter'd robes!
> (V.v.61–69)

Yet while we admire Edward, we cannot avoid the impression that his endurance is more a matter of fact than a matter of will.

The King doesn't affirm life by surviving, but rather like a concentration camp prisoner endures while longing for death.

Similarly, an heroic stoicism pervades Young Mortimer's last speech.

> Base Fortune, now I see, that in thy wheel
> There is a point, to which when men aspire,
> They tumble headlong down. That point I touch'd.
> And seeing there was no place to mount up higher,
> Why should I grieve at my declining fall?
>   (V.vi.59–63)

Yet his final words in this speech are inappropriate—more bravado than sincere:

> Farewell, fair Queen, weep not for Mortimer,
> That scorns the world, and as a traveller
> Goes to discover countries yet unknown.
>   (V.vi.64–66)

Nothing in the play indicates Mortimer's scorn for the world or his quest for new experience; this sort of speech is appropriate to Tennyson's "Ulysses," but is irrelevant to Mortimer.

As indicated at the beginning, *Edward II* does have impact. It is a play with a certain eternal modernity; the conflict between new and old in itself speaks to each generation. When this conflict turns out to raise a more basic question—whether any system, person, change makes a difference—the play becomes wonderfully contemporary.

3

Juliet's Question and Shakespeare's Names

Murray J. Levith

The poet's eye, in a fine frenzy rolling,
Doth glance from heaven to earth, from earth to heaven;
And as imagination bodies forth
The forms of things unknown, the poet's pen
Turns them to shapes, and gives to aery nothing
A local habitation and a name.
           A Midsummer Night's Dream (V.i.12–17)

Some of Shakespeare's most familiar lines occur during the balcony scene in *Romeo and Juliet* when Juliet asks a hidden Romeo to "refuse" his name. "'Tis but thy name that is my enemy," she reasons. "O, be some other name!" There follows Juliet's famous question: "What's in a name?"[1]

Her answer is that there is nothing in a name:

                    That which we call a rose
By any other word [Quarto 1 has "name"] would smell as sweet.
So Romeo would, were he not Romeo call'd,

1. (II.ii.34,38,42). All references to the plays are quoted from *The Riverside Shakespeare,* edited by G. Blakemore Evans (Boston: Houghton Mifflin, 1974), and will appear parenthetically in the text.

21

Retain that dear perfection which he owes
Without that title.

(II.ii.43–7)

Juliet to the contrary, however, names mean a lot—especially in
Shakespeare.

Books explaining names in the Classics and the Bible began
appearing in England toward the end of the fifteenth century.
Late in the sixteenth century one William Patten published his
exhaustively titled *The Calendar of Scripture, Wherein the Hebru,
Calldian, Arabian, Phenician, Syrian, Persian, Greek and Latin
names, of Nations, Cuntreys, Men, Weemen, Idols, Cities; Hils,
Riuers, & of oother places in the holly Byble mentioned, by order
of letters ar set, and turned into oour English Toong* (STC 19476).
In his "*Praefatio*" to *De Sapientia Veterum*, Francis Bacon explains that the ancients chose names for the characters of their
fables most deliberately: "*cum Metis uxor Jovis plane consilium
sonet; Typhon tumorem; Pan universum; Nemesis vindictam: et
similia.*"[2] Elizabethan and Jacobean dramatists were often obvious
with character names, as for example Ben Jonson in *Volpone*.
William Camden's 1605 *Remaines* (STC 4521) and the 1607 revision of *Britannia* (STC 4508) included glossaries to explain both
men's and women's names from Anglo-Saxon roots, as well as from
Hebrew, Greek, and Latin. Camden observes in *Remaines* "that
names among all nations and tongues . . . are significative, and
not vaine senselesse sounds." He cites examples even to "the bar-
barous Turks," "the savages of *Hispaniola* and all *America*," and
"they of *Congo*." Thus, he concludes, "it were grosse ignorance
and to no small reproach of our Progenitours, to think their names
onely nothing significative, because that in the daily alteration of
our tong, the signification of them is lost, or not commonly
knowne" (pp. 36–37).

Not until the nineteenth century, however, does the deliber-
ateness of Shakespeare's names begin to attract notice. Perhaps
this aspect of the playwright's art seemed too obvious to men-

2. *The Works of Francis Bacon*, edited by James Spedding, Robert Leslie Ellis,
Douglas Denon Heath (Boston: Brown and Taggard, 1860), XII, 429.

tion earlier. In any case, it was not until December of 1862 that John Ruskin published sections from his *Munera Pulveris*, a treatise on political economy, which in asides and footnotes attempted to explain the significance of some of Shakespeare's names. Ruskin notes that names in Shakespeare "are curiously—often barbarously—much by Providence,—but assuredly not without Shakespeare's cunning purpose—mixed out of the various traditions he confusedly adopted, and languages which he imperfectly knew."[3] Focusing on etymology, Ruskin explains Desdemona as meaning "miserable fortune," Othello as "the careful," Ophelia "serviceableness," Hamlet "homely," Hermione "pillar-like," Titania "the queen," Benedick and Beatrice "blessed" and "blessing," Valentine and Proteus "enduring" and "changeful," and Iago and Iachimo both "the supplanter." In another section, Ruskin relates Portia to "fortune's lady," Perdita to "lost lady," and Cordelia to "heart-lady." Ruskin promised a full-length study of Shakespeare's names at some later date, but it never materialized. Perhaps the reason for this was Matthew Arnold's scathing criticism of Ruskin's first efforts.

Arnold responded to Ruskin's excursions on Shakespearean nomenclature with feigned or real outrage. In *The Cornhill Magazine*, he summarizes Ruskin's work with a sentence of dismissal: "Now, really, what a piece of extravagance all this is!"[4] Taking Ruskin to task for faulty etymologies and especially for giving Shakespeare's names undue prominence, Arnold accuses Ruskin of being unbalanced and, undoubtedly worst of all, provincial. Perhaps this severity of rebuke deterred interest in Shakespeare's names until quite recently.

G. Wilson Knight revives Juliet's question in a chapter in *The Soverign Flower*, and his study is provocative and often insightful.[5] Knight's ear is especially tuned to the poetic suggestiveness of Shakespeare's names. He notices, for example, the power conveyed by the *o*'s in Oberon, Morocco, Othello, Orsino, and, con-

3. *The Crown of Wild Olives* (New York: U.S. Book Co., nd), VIII, 200–202. Ruskin's observations on Shakespeare's names were first published in *Fraser's Magazine* (December 1862):742–56, and (April 1863):441–62.
4. See the entire article in 10 (August 1864):154–172.
5. (London: Methuen, 1958), pp. 161–201.

versely, the "certain lightness" of "Ophelia's name, with its rising vowel-sounds from 'o' through 'e' to 'i'." Knight is always interesting even when he seems far afield, as for example with the names Yorick and Osric. He writes that contained in these names "may be an overtone of 'joke': one *made* jokes, the other *is* a joke."

Harry Levin has written another chapter on the subject.[6] He acknowledges the worth of Knight's study, though recognizing its limitations. Levin is a bit more careful than Knight, but in the end goes over much the same ground. Levin's work does, however, offer an appealing invitation for further study of Juliet's question: "Except for one or two German dissertations, which are hardly more than annotated listings, plus a few articles on specific lines of derivation, the field of Shakespearean nomenclature is wide open, and constitutes an inviting pasture to browse in."

Shakespeare himself is on record in *A Midsummer Night's Dream* concerning the poetic process: the poet "gives to aery nothing / A local habitation and a name" (V.i.16–17). Although one might wish to define "name" here in a general sense, one can be quite literal as well. The name attached to a Shakespearean character can be a basic dramatic and poetic image. This is not to say that all of the playwright's names are meaningful or significative. It does little good to "find" meaning where none has been intended. On the other hand, however, names are often tonal and provide significant reading directions—clues to thematic meanings and characterizations. In some cases Shakespeare was limited by names inherited from source materials. Nevertheless, in such instances he might build characterization consistent with the suggestiveness of a received name. "Hotspur" comes first to mind in this regard. Presumably Shakespeare read the name in Holinshed and then created an impulsive, impetuous, and choleric personality to go with the name. The playwright's invented names, too, are often similarly linked to characterization. This is easiest to observe in his denotative or "tag" names.

For the most part dealing with minor and especially comic characters and secondary play actions, Shakespeare will single out

6. "Shakespeare's Nomenclature," in *Essays on Shakespeare,* edited by Gerald W. Chaptman (Princeton, N.J.: Princeton University Press, 1965), pp. 59–90.

a vivid attribute and so label a character, either by occupation, physical trait or feature, or some notable aspect of personality.

Sir Oliver *Martext* is a country priest in *As You Like It*. The Mistresses Quickly, Overdone, and Doll Tearsheet have names clearly associated with their bawdy business. Abhorson's name is a portmanteau of "abhor" and "whoreson" and seems apt for an executioner. Another executioner, Richard II's, is Sir Pierce (of Exton). Brakenbury (*break* and *bury*) is the Lieutenant of the Tower in *Richard III*. Some of the thieving crew in the *Henry IV* plays also have occupational tag names. "Gadshill" comes from the notorious place of highway robbery, Gads Hill, on the road between London and Kent near Rochester. "Peto" is from *petard*, literally a "small weapon." Pistol's name is obvious. Fang, whose name means to "capture" or "catch," assisted properly by Snare, arrests Falstaff. In like manner, but perhaps named a bit more subtly, are the rude mechanicals of *A Midsummer Night's Dream*. Quince and Snug are carpenters, as "quince" or "quines" are blocks of wood to be joined "snugly." Bottom is a weaver, and his name is a reference to the spool, core, or "bottom" of a skein upon which thread or yarn is wound. The bellows mender Flute has the job of repairing the fluted stops of church organs which whistle when they have holes in them. Tinkers solder spouts or snouts to metal pitchers, and this is Tom Snout's occupation. Robin Starveling is a tailor whose traditional work posture suggests a bird-like pose.

But Snout, Starveling, and Bottom are named also for intended physical features as well. Snout is presumably long-nosed, Starveling must have a thin physique, and Bottom a broad seat. Additionally, Quince might be small and wizened like the fruit.

Other characters in Shakespeare are similarly named. In *The Comedy of Errors*, Dr. Pinch has his name from a slight build. He is described as "a hungry lean-fac'd villain, / A mere anatomy . . . / A needy, hollow-ey'd, sharp-looking wretch, / A living dead man" (V.i.238–42). Another frail character is Sir Andrew Aguecheek whose family name means "fever cheek." Slender is thin of both girth and wit. On the other hand, though diminutive in size, the Moth of *Love's Labor's Lost* is not so in brains. Another tiny Moth appears in *A Midsummer Night's Dream*, together with the other fairies, Peaseblossom, Cobweb, and Mustardseed, whose names indicate their forest habitation and their size. Physical traits figure also in the naming of the recruits in *2 Henry IV*. Says Falstaff of the "mouldy" Mouldy, "it is time you were spent" (III.ii.117). Shadow is a mere shadow of a man (III.ii.126–35). The names Feeble, Wart, and Bullcalf, too, are obvious indicators of physical features or attributes. Justice Shallow is named for his mental endowment, as is Simple and Simpcox. Silence doesn't speak much. And, of course, Sir Toby.

Most of the tag names in the plays are English, but some are not. The setting of *All's Well That Ends Well* is sometimes French, and we find in this play the "fiery" Lafew and the "wordy" Parolles. Even when a setting isn't French, one may have a "strong-armed" Fortinbras, or a French queen Cordelia with a noble "heart of a lion." The Spanish word for *drunkard* yields Borachio's name. When the setting is Italian, we encounter the "blond" Biondello or the "white" and "pure" Bianca of *The Taming of the Shrew*. Malvolio is ill-willed and Benvolio is good-willed in keeping with the meanings of their names.

Shakespeare creates a special group of tag names in the Romances, the meanings of which he explains in the plays themselves. Miranda denotes the "admirable" or the "wonderful," and Ferdinand addresses his love at one point as "Admir'd Miranda" (III.i.37) and at another exclaims "O you wonder!" (I.ii.427). Miranda herself cries "O wonder!" in the dialogue (V.i.182). Marina, in *Pericles*, explains that she was "Call'd Marina / For I was born at sea" (V.i.155–56). Hermione asks that her newly born be named Perdita in *The Winter's Tale*, "for the babe / Is counted lost for ever" (III.iii.32–33).

The playwright uses tag names at times ironically in terms of character. *Othello* seems consciously structured with irony in mind—black is good, white is bad—and in it there appears the courtesan Bianca. Angelo of *Measure for Measure* is certainly no angel. Neither is Angelica, Juliet's garrulous nurse. We might expect a sharper Launce than we get in *Two Gentlemen of Verona*. A bit dull also is Launcelot Gobbo of *The Merchant of Venice*.

One other sort of denotative name occurs in Shakespeare.

While Seyton is a legitimate Scottish clan name, it contains the unmistakable overtone of the devil's designation. As the central character in a psychomachian allegory, Macbeth has lost his soul to the forces of Evil, and it is most appropriate for him to have Seyton (Satan) as his only attendant at the end (V.iii.29 is Seyton's first entrance). Another character named in the manner of the old allegories and moralities is Patience, woman to noble Queen Katherine in *Henry VIII*.

Unfortunately not all of Shakespeare's tag names are obvious to the modern reader or playgoer. In some cases, significant denotation has become obscured due to normal language change, and can be recovered only with the help of historical dictionaries like the *Oxford English Dictionary*. Nym's name, for example, under "nim" in the *OED*, meant "to steal" in colloquial jargon; in *Henry V* Nym is hanged for looting French churches. With foreign names the problem of tag meanings is compounded. John Florio's copious Italian-English dictionary, *A Worlde of Wordes*, and its expanded editions is helpful for Italian names.[7] Florio was tutor to Shakespeare's patron, the Earl of Southampton, and it seems likely he knew the playwright. Indeed, one theory speculates that the pedant Holofernes, whose name is an inexact anagram of the dictionary-maker's, is meant to be a satiric portrait of him. Florio translates the word *stefano:* "hath been used in jest for a mans bellie, panch, craver, mawe, or gut," and this definition helps to characterize Stephano, the King of Naples' drunken butler in *The Tempest*. Florio also offers clues as to how a character might be played in terms of his given name. Thus we have *Peto*, "one that doth lightly roule his eies with a grace from corner to corner, goat-eied, rouling-eied, also he that looketh as his eies were halfe closed, or he that looketh a squint upward." *Bardo* as "light nimble, bould, saucie" similarly points to the personality of the thief Bardolph. William Camden's glossaries, too, are contemporary aids for establishing what a name might have suggested to Shakespeare or his audience. Camden defines Edgar as "*Happy,*

7. The first edition appeared in 1598, but was expanded in 1611 with the new title *Queen Anna's New World of Words, or Dictionarie of the Italian and English Tongues*. George Torriano further expanded it in 1688 and called it simply *A Dictionary, Italian and English*.

or *blessed honor,* or *power,*" and Edmund is "Happy, or blessed peace." In the case of the later name, S. Musgrove suggests that Shakespeare's eye might have noticed what follows for *Edmund* in Camden: "Our Lawyers yet doe acknowledge *Mund* for *Peace* in their word *Mundbrech,* for breach of *Peace.*" Camden also explains Oswald as "House-ruler or Steward."[8]

Some of Shakespeare's character names allude to similarly named figures in mythology, literature, the Bible, history, or some other familiar source. Such allusion serves oftentimes to delineate character rapidly or may have a comic function. Autolycus, Mercury's thieving son in Ovid, explains himself as such in *The Winter's Tale:* "My father nam'd me Autolycus, who being, as I am, litter'd under Mercury, was likewise a snapper-up of unconsider'd trifles" (IV.iii.24–26). The juxtaposition of the names Rowland, Orlando, and Oliver in *As You Like It* recalls the famous *Chanson de Roland.* Aaron and Jessica are both outsiders in their plays, and Shakespeare found their names in the Old Testament. The playwright was especially fond of giving his servant characters out-sized allusive names. Thus we have Sampson in *Romeo and Juliet,* and Alexander in *Troilus and Cressida.* Another comic device was to give characters oxymoronic names—fine ones contradicted by mean ones. Here we might list Christopher Sly, Anthony Dull, and Pompey Bum, among others. For these names, Shakespeare's typical pattern is to couple an allusion in the Christian name with a denotative tag in the family name.

Shakespeare accords animal names to some of his characters, and these can be denotative, allusive, or both. There are a surprising number of such names. "Lavatch" corresponds to the French words for "the cow." While literally referring to the fruit of the dogwood tree, "Dogberry" also recalls the animal, lovable but severely limited in intelligence. Sometimes to the chagrin of other characters in his play, the constable Dogberry is too "dogged" in his interrogations and investigations, and his use of language smacks of "doggerel." Talbot's name recalls the fierce hunting hound, ancestor of the present day bloodhound. (Chaucer's dog in the "Nun's Priest's Tale" is "Talbot.") In *1 Henry VI,* Tal-

8. See "The Nomenclature of *King Lear,*" *Review of English Studies* 7 (1956):294–295.

bot comments that the French call the English "dogs" "for our fierceness" (I.v.25). The Bastard of Orleance views the fiery Talbot as a hell hound: "I think this Talbot be a fiend of Hell" (II.i.46). The names "Tybalt" and "Reynaldo" are both to be found in the medieval story of *Reynard the Fox*. "Tybalt" is the cat's name. In *Romeo and Juliet*, the sharp-tongued Mercutio calls Tybalt a "rat-catcher" and the "King of Cats" (III.i.75,77), drawing attention to the allusion contained in his name. Polonius' servant's name, "Reynaldo," is an obvious allusion to the sly fox Reynard himself. Reynaldo's mission in *Hamlet* is to act covertly in order to discover Laertes' behavior and reputation while he is abroad. Petruchio's successful wooing changes Kate from a "wildcat" to a "cate" (meaning "delicacy"). He says to her early on: "I am he born to tame you, Kate, / And bring you from a wild Kate to a Kate / Conformable as other household Kates" (II.i.276–78).

In 1596 Sir John Harington published a widely circulated Rabelaisian book with the innocent title *The Metamorphosis of Ajax*.[9] Among other things, the book turns out to be an announcement of the invention of the flush toilet which Harington refers to as "a jax." The name "Ajax" soon became synonymous with *privy* in the contemporary idiom. Since foul smells associated with privies were thought to result in melancholy, Shakespeare's Ajax in *Troilus and Cressida*, described as "melancholy without cause" (I.ii.26), must have brought howls of laughter just because of his name and disposition. The same name association obtains for Jaques in *As You Like It*. Jaquenetta, the damsel in *Love's Labor's Lost*, has a name which is a French feminine diminutive of "Jaques," and perhaps is meant to contain a reference to the smell of the country wench. Rendered in English "Jaques" is, of course, "Jack," the popular nickname for "John" (slang for toilet). Following this logic, Don John in *Much Ado About Nothing* is deliberately named for his temperament. As the anti-romantic villain in a romantic comedy, his name points to his melancholic nature. Surely he is no Don Juan or Don Giovanni. "Iago," too, spanish for "James," is a variant of the French "Jacques." Santiago, St. James, the patron saint of Spain, recalled for Shakespeare's

9. The modern edition of the work was edited by Elizabeth Story Donno (New York: Columbia University Press, 1962).

contemporaries the name invoked in the war cry of the Spanish Armada. Iago's name might thus be thought to link a disposition for melancholy to a motivation for evil. Similarly, Jachimo's name is a clue to his temperament, "Jachimo" being a diminutive of "Iago."

With recent history, allusion was not always without hazards: Oldcastle's descendants were alive to complain and necessitate a name change. In *The Merry Wives of Windsor*, "Brooke" is an appropriate wet alias for "Ford," but the name had to be watered down to a dry "Broome" for the Folio to avoid offending the Seventh Lord Cobham, William *Brooke*. Ancient history, too, could inhibit creativity if classical tradition dictated that "Cressida" might only be Cressida.

On the other hand, however, there was room for great allusive subtlety. The name "Theseus" in *A Midsummer Night's Dream* triggers a recollection of the Minotaur myth. In Shakespeare's play Bottom, the fabulous ass-man, is found in the center of a forest-labyrinth to which the youths and maidens come. Invited to get to the "bottom" of "this most rare vision" of plays within plays and dreams within dreams, Shakespeare's audience need clutch only at the thread of the meaning of Bottom's name, a weaver's spool, what Theseus used to defeat the Minotaur.

Similarly, a saint's legend might be invoked with a given name, and have interpretive value for a play. In *The Merchant of Venice*, for example, the title character Antonio's name recalls two well-known saints, St. Anthony the Great and St. Anthony of Padua. According to legend, St. Anthony the Great, like Anthony the merchant, showed remarkable patience when faced with many trials, and he was an ascetic all of his life. Relics of this Saint are in Vienne in France, a place name curiously similar to the Venice of Shakespeare's title setting. Even more to the point of Shakespeare's play, perhaps, is the legend of the other St. Anthony. He is patron of the poor, as is the generous merchant for Bassanio. This St. Anthony's life contains a central episode concerning the conversion of a Jew. As the story goes, after many unsuccessful attempts to convert the man St. Anthony declared that a wild ass would sooner honor the Sacrament. A few days later, however, while the Saint was on his way to minister to a dying man, an ass left a stable and knelt before Anthony. The report of this miracle led to the conversion of many.

Henry VIII affords us yet another instance of allusive subtlety in Shakespeare's use of names. Here the playwright uses source names from history but exploits them in a manner which enriches the thematic material of his play. Anne Bullen's Christian name corresponds with the name of St. Ann, mother of the Virgin Mary. Anne's child Elizabeth, then, is associated through allusion with the Virgin Queen of Heaven. Elizabeth, of course, was remembered by the audience for *Henry VIII* as the Virgin Queen of Earth. In the same play, the holy maiden St. Catherine is also invoked. The spiked wheel or "Catherine's Wheel" associated with her martyrdom picks up the pervasive Wheel of Fortune motif in the play. Moreover, the Saint's legend adds an additional dimension to the character of the patient, noble, and wronged Queen Katherine.

Finally, *King John* provides one further example of name allusion in Shakespeare's plays. The name "John" has not been especially favored among English kings. Rather, "Arthur," "Richard," and "Henry" seem the most popular royal names, especially for the periods of history Shakespeare treats in his plays. But all four names are to be found in *King John*. The reason is that one of Shakespeare's themes is kingship and its various aspects. "John" is the designation for a bad king, "Richard" (recalling the "Lionhearted") a brave one, "Arthur" the legendary, and "Henry" the good governor of a great empire. In the play, the Bastard changes his given name "Philip," associated more with French kings than English, to "Richard" after his father Richard the Lionhearted.

Shakespeare's own name is composed of double English syllables, "shake" and "spear," and a number of the playwright's characters have similarly formulated names: Falstaff, Hotspur, Shylock, Touchstone. What is remarkable here is the importance of these characters to their plays. None is a protagonist but all are central figures.

What about some of the more poetic aspects of Shakespearean nomenclature? A reader merely rehearsing the *dramatis personae* of *Othello*—Othello, Desdemona, Iago, Cassio—knows from the sounds of the names that this will not be a comedy. A chorus of women, maiden, mate, and mother, is suggested by the alliterated names in *Coriolanus:* Valeria, Virgilia, Volumnia. In *The Merchant of Venice,* Salanio, Salarino, and Salario are a male chorus. Shakespeare again exploits alliteration in order to juxtapose characters for comparison or contrast: Hotspur and Hal, Edgar and Edmund, Richard and Richmond, Macbeth and Macduff, Beatrice and Benedick. The indistinguishable false friends of Hamlet are Rosencrantz and Guildenstern whose names jingle together. Richard II's favorites, Bushy, Bagot, and Greene, have names which, taken together with the mentioned but not seen Wiltshire, suggest an uncared for garden. The allegory of the garden scene in the play *Richard II* is underlined by such character naming, and Bullingbrook makes it explicit when he refers to "Bushy, Bagot and their complices, /. . . [as] The caterpillars of the commonwealth, / Which I have sworn to weed and pluck away" (II.iii.165–67). *Henry V* also has deliberate naming in it. The Welsh Fluellen together with the Irish MacMorris and the Scottish Jamy are meant to reflect the diversity of King Henry's subjects and suggest a British microcosm.

While patterns in Shakespeare's naming of characters can be observed and analyzed, there also arise some baffling questions to which satisfactory answers may never be forthcoming. Why, for example, are there two Jaques and two Olivers in *As You Like It?* Why two dissimilar characters in a play both with the name Bardolph? Why a conjuror with Henry IV's family name Bolingbrook? Why two Eglamours? Why a minor middle man Claudio in *Hamlet* (IV.vii.40) when Claudius is such an important character? Why so many Antonios in the plays? Why so many names beginning with the syllable "Luc-"?

As the nurse tells us, Juliet is named for her birth month (I.iii.21), and we have left her poised on the balcony with her question. As we recall, she has asked the still hidden Romeo to "doff" his offendingly meaningful name. "Who's there," Juliet wants to know when she hears something below. The perplexed Romeo can only respond amusingly: "By a name, / I know not how to tell thee who I am."

4

Milton's "I's": The Narrator and the Reader in *Paradise Lost*

ROGER B. ROLLIN

> . . . there is nothing either good or bad, but thinking makes it so.
> *Hamlet* (II.ii.255–56)

> The mind is its own place, and in it self
> Can make a Heav'n of Hell, a Hell of Heav'n
> *Paradise Lost* (I.254–55)

> The Freudian psychology is the only systematic account of the human mind which in point of subtlety and complexity, of interest and tragic power, deserves to stand beside the chaotic mass of psychological insights which literature has accumulated through the centuries; . . . of all mental systems, the Freudian psychology is the one which makes poetry indigenous to the very constitution of the mind. Indeed, the mind, as Freud sees it, is in the greater part of its tendency exactly a poetry-making organ.
> Lionel Trilling, "Freud and Literature"

P*aradise Lost* is not only an act of mind; it is itself a kind of mental "system" upon which the ego-system of its reader, functioning at all levels, draws. Product of the mind of John Milton,

Paradise Lost is both less than that mind—which was conscious of more than ever found its way into the poem—and more than that mind—containing within its psychological "deep structure" materials of which John Milton could not have been conscious. A reader of *Paradise Lost*, whose own ego-system functions both consciously and unconsciously, thus encounters what might be described as an artificial (esthetic) "psychical personality." Between that inert but potentially dynamic "personality" and the psychical personality of the reader a "transaction" takes place, one which has widely varying potentialities for contributing to the ongoing creation and re-creation of the reader's personal identity. This process is summarized by Norman N. Holland as follows: "A reader responds to a literary work by assimilating it to his own psychological processes, that is, to his search for successful solutions within his identity theme to the multiple demands, both inner and outer, on his ego."[1] My essay will indicate how Holland's model of the dynamics of literary response (*Readers*, Chapter 5) bears upon two current critical controversies concerning *Paradise Lost* and upon possibilities for further study of the poem. One of the controversies to be discussed has been erupting sporadically ever since William Blake read Milton. It centers upon the question, "Who is the hero of *Paradise Lost?*" The other controversy, concerning the nature and functions of the narrator of Milton's epic, has surfaced more recently.

That the problem of the narrator of *Paradise Lost* and the problem of its hero are linked has been suggested by William G. Riggs. Reacting against the "poetless poem" of New Criticism, and emphasizing the apparently autobiographical passages of the epic, the "Puritan inclination to autobiography," and Milton's heroic conception of the poet, Riggs concludes that the true hero of *Paradise Lost* is the narrator himself. That narrator, Riggs continues, is in fact John Milton or at least John Milton's conception

1. *Five Readers Reading* (New Haven, Conn.: Yale University Press, 1975), p. 128—cited in my text as *Readers*.

of himself.[2] Riggs tries to steer his critical course between the Scylla of simplistic autobiographical reading and the Charybdis of rigorously Formalistic reading.[3] The latter views the narrator only as a *character* who has been *invented* by the poet, "a special voice designed to express Milton's special interpretation of Adam's Fall" (*Milton's Epic Voice*, p. 179). That voice has its heroic pitch, Anne Davidson Ferry acknowledges (*Milton's Epic Voice*, p. 181), but her emphasis is upon the narrator as blind bard, one who is in a sense outside the world of the poem because that world exists only as it is interpreted for readers by him. Thus Ferry de-emphasizes the "dramatic" qualities of *Paradise Lost*, preferring to concentrate upon the poem as narrative.

There are undoubtedly merits to this argument. The blind bard of *Paradise Lost* and the blind Milton cannot be identical. Subjectivity expressed is subjectivity altered; the medium must modify the message. However resolute an author's intention, achieving an identity between his subjectivity and the "objectivity" of his expression must be beyond him. Ultimately, the logic of the literary mode demands that the narrator in *Paradise Lost* be viewed as a fictional character created by John Milton for specific esthetic purposes, and as one who bears only those relationships to John Milton the man which John Milton the poet allows.[4] Such "allowance" will be the result of some conscious, some unconscious choices, and each type of choice can bear the stamp of a different aspect of John Milton's psychical personality. Thus, when Riggs suggests that in *Paradise Lost* "the pressure of autobiography is a shaping factor" (*The Christian Poet*, p. 3), he is close to the truth, except that "autobiography" implies that the "shaping" is more or less conscious. From a psychoanalytic point

2. *The Christian Poet* in Paradise Lost (Berkeley, Calif.: University of California Press, 1972), pp. 4–7—cited in text as *The Christian Poet*.
3. For him represented by Denis Surat, *Milton, Man and Thinker* (New York: Dial, 1925), and by Anne Davidson Ferry, *Milton's Epic Voice: The Narrator in Paradise Lost* (Cambridge, Mass.: Harvard University Press, 1967)—cited in text as *Milton's Epic Voice*.
4. I have argued this point at more length in "*Paradise Lost*: Tragical-Comical-Historical-Pastoral," in *Milton Studies*, V edited by James D. Simmonds (Pittsburgh, Pa.: University of Pittsburgh Press, 1974), pp. 3–37.

of view it would be more accurate and more meaningful to substitute the term "ego" for "autobiography," for then Riggs's statement would accommodate a factor which both he and Ferry neglect—that any discussion of the narrator of *Paradise Lost* must take into account not only the demands of the literary form itself and the poet's *conscious* responses to those demands, but his *unconscious* responses as well.

When Professor Ferry insists upon viewing *Paradise Lost* as essentially a narrative poem she is on firm but limited ground; since every one of its 10,565 lines is the "utterance" of a blind bard, Milton's epic technically lacks even the most rudimentary requisites for the dramatic mode. Yet generations of readers have testified to its "dramatic" power, and that power derives in part from the very aspect of the poem upon which Professor Ferry has focused her attention—the narrator. For like a skillful playwright, Milton activates the interest of his audience and their involvement through a calculatedly gradual development of the narrator's character—for example, by revealing him to be a bard and potential "culture hero" in the invocation to Book I, but not revealing that he is a *blind* bard and thus all the more heroic until the invocation to Book III. Furthermore, contrary to Professor Ferry, the presence of this narrator neither technically nor practically need inhibit audience response to the poem's "dramatic" dimension, for characters serving as prologs, envoys, and "stage managers" have comprised a convention of the theater from its beginnings down to the present. And whether they have functioned outside the action or within it they have clearly proved no bar to audiences experiencing such works as plays.

Finally, Milton not only presents his persona as a dramatic character, but makes him the protagonist of a dramatic sub-plot which frames *Paradise Lost,* a kind of "play-beyond-the-play" centering upon the struggle of an alienated and oppressed artist to compose a great poem. This "monodrama" is in four "acts"— the invocations to Books I, III, VII, and IX. There is no fifth and final act, for the brilliant dénouement that is the last forty-three lines of Book XII serves as the implied climax of the blind bard's plot, *prima facie* evidence that the poet-hero has completed his superhuman task.

To classify the narrator as a hero is to approach the position taken by Professor Riggs. It is, however, necessary to note the fact that after Book IX this hero is removed from center stage, which suggests that the resolution of "dramas" other than the monodrama of the blind bard apparently was for Milton a more pressing concern. As I have argued elsewhere (on structural grounds), and as I will argue in this essay (on psychoanalytic grounds), Milton's narrator is indeed a hero-figure, but only one of *several* hero-figures in the poem.[5]

The notion of multiple heroes has most recently received consideration from John T. Shawcross, who asserts that "One of Milton's aims in *Paradise Lost* is to achieve a spectrum of heroic action and its antithesis."[6] His interesting conclusion is that the true hero of the epic is "every man who follows the path to life as laid out in the poem"; that is, readers who finally submit to Eternal Providence and acknowledge the just ways of God to men. To posit as hero for the poem one who is "outside" the actual plot of the poem is a hypothesis which, carried to its logical conclusion, allows for the possibility that among the true heroes of *Paradise Lost* could be those who had never read *Paradise Lost;* surely it is following "the path to life as laid out in the poem," not the mere reading of the poem, that must be the *sine qua non* of this type of heroism. Nonetheless, there is a sense in which *all* readers are, at least theoretically, "within" *Paradise Lost,* for their lives are wholly circumscribed by the epic's time-space continuum, which stretches from the creation of the world (as described in Book VII) to its final destruction (as prophesied in Book XII).

5. *Ibid.*
6. "The Hero of *Paradise Lost* One More Time," a paper presented at the University of Wisconsin–Milwaukee Milton Tercentenary Conference, November 1974, abstracted in *Milton Quarterly* 9 (March, 1975):36. It should be pointed out that although Professor Shawcross and I agree that Milton's poem has more than a single hero he is in implicit disagreement with my conclusions as set forth in my abovementioned article. Shawcross views Satan as an anti-hero rather than a tragic hero; regards Adam and Eve not as heroes of a pastoral tragicomedy, but as protagonists of a kind of morality play; and perceives Christ as a "prototype" rather than as an "historical" hero.

Another recent attempt to resolve the problem of the reader and *Paradise Lost* is that of John R. Mulder.[7] His hypothesis, perhaps the most radical yet proposed, holds Milton's narrator to be if not a downright villain, at least an untrustworthy source of the true meaning of the epic, and certainly no hero figure. In fact, Mulder argues, the narrator and his God are meant by Milton to be *rejected* by the readers of *Paradise Lost*. Mulder thus stands directly opposed to the interpretation of Stanley Fish who (like Riggs and Ferry) sees the narrator as heroic and who (like Shawcross) sees the reader as also heroic, though only within the "sphere of action" of the poem and only after the reader has been "surprised" by his own sin.[8] Like many other Miltonists Fish also believes that the poet "secures a positive response to the figure of God" (*Surprised by Sin,* p. 70) from his readers. Thus is the issue joined.

Since it is unlikely, Professor Mulder argues, that a poet who disliked monarchy and messianism "should have intended a messianic poem about a monarchical god," and since that God is wholly beyond justification, being nothing more than the deification of raw power and brute force, He and the politically and morally blind bard who is his apologist must both be rejected by sensitive readers. It is not the teller who is to be trusted, but the tale, and that tale is a horror story, an implicit exposé of Christianity's inhumanity to man, and the inhumanity of all such hierarchical power structures. If we observe Milton's entire "composition from the *outside*" instead of trusting ourselves to the "inside" view, that of the narrator, we will, Mulder suggests, read *Paradise Lost* ironically, as a condemnation of God's (and Caesar's) ways to men: "ruin is the praise of power."

Even setting the Intentional Fallacy aside, to argue that Milton could not have been inconsistent on so grand a scale may oversimplify the phenomenon of creativity; all the extant evidence, both clinical and anecdotal, confirms the vital role that unconscious impulses play in the creative process. Unpremeditated

7. "The Pied Piper and the Great Whale," a paper presented at the University of Wisconsin–Milwaukee Milton Tercentenary Conference, November 1974.
8. Stanley E. Fish, *Surprised by Sin: The Reader in Paradise Lost* (Berkeley, Calif.: University of California Press, 1971); cited in the text as *Surprised by Sin*.

verse can owe much to Latin Secretaries as well as to ambitious
blind bards. Celestial patronesses are, after all, brokers in a form
of power. Nor is it necessary to urge readers to observe *Paradise
Lost* from the outside, from the perspective of their post-Miltonic
selves, rather than from the internal perspective of the Miltonic
narrator; the fact is that readers do both. Only psychotic person-
alities are regularly incapable of distinguishing fantasy from
reality. Just as children routinely make distinctions between their
play and real life, adults (as Freud has pointed out) distinguish
between their fantasies, literature included, and reality.[9] Neither
Milton's narrator nor the narrative of *Paradise Lost* itself is likely
to displace for any longer than the normal attention span the ma-
teriality of readers and of their environments.

On the other hand, as sensitive readers know, to make ex-
cessively scrupulous and constant distinctions between the text
and one's environment is to doom the esthetic experience. For a
reading of *Paradise Lost* to be successful, i.e., pleasurable, a willing suspension of disbelief is a prerequisite. Prerequisite even to
that state, though it is frequently overlooked by sophisticated
critics, is the inhibition of our motor activity. For to read such a
poem as *Paradise Lost* requires that we *lower* our state of readi-
ness for acting upon external reality. "To be active in the inner
world," as Norman Holland points out, "we must be passive toward the outer, for action binds us to reality."[10] Being required
to *act* physically and verbally during most of our waking hours,
in literature we are afforded an opportunity only to *react*, to perform private, mental transactions. Indeed, Milton's narrator asks
no more of his auditors than that they *listen* to his great argument, and that only by implication; *Paradise Lost* is, like "Lycidas," a poem "overheard." The narrator's pious hope that those
who do "overhear" will act, will change their lives, can be inferred
from his speeches. But at most he implicitly asks for their reac-

9. Sigmund Freud, "Creative Writers and Day-Dreaming," *The Complete Psychological Works of Sigmund Freud* IX (1906–1908), edited and translated by James
Strachey *et al.* (London: The Hogarth Press and The Institute of Psychoanalysis,
1959), pp. 143–53.
10. *The Dynamics of Literary Response* (New York: Oxford University Press,
1968), pp. 73–74—cited in text as *Dynamics*.

tion, for their submission to Eternal Providence and their acqui-
escence to God's ways towards men. Thus, although Professors
Fish and Shawcross may envision *Paradise Lost* as, among other
things, an esthetic system for making real-life heroes, Milton's
narrator is more restrained in his aims—and also more in accord
with the accumulated evidence concerning art's efficacy in alter-
ing human behavior. It would seem that by the time he reached
his fifties, even the author of *Areopagitica* had become less san-
guine about the power of books.

To review: the normal ego-function of reality-testing is to
some extent suppressed when readers read, and this, plus their
minimized motor activity, licenses their passive "fusion" with the
text. In the case of night-dreams or daydreams such a state could
be described by the clinical term "regressive," connoting, in Holland's words, "a level of mental functioning lower than one's ordinary level" (*Dynamics,* pp. 81–82). But, in reading a work like
Paradise Lost, "while we reach down to our earliest, most primitive state of merger with our gratifications, we still retain some of
our highest levels of mental functioning." Here it should be
stressed that terms like "regressive," "lower," and "higher" seem
as if they are value laden, but such is not Holland's intention;
rather, he sees clinical evidence as supportive of the traditional
view that reading is—to use a non-traditional phrase—a "con-
sciousness-raising activity." And as reading extends our mental
and emotional ranges, adaptation is enhanced; a work such as
Paradise Lost "allows us to loosen boundaries—between self and
not-self, inner and outer, past, present, and future" (*Dynamics,*
p. 101). To put the matter in yet another way, *Paradise Lost* can
expand its readers' "mythic consciousness" without also displac-
ing their "linear consciousness."

One of the processes by which such effects are achieved in
readers' minds is that of identification with literary characters
like Milton's narrator, Satan, Adam, and Eve. Of these characters,
the narrator is surely, in Louis Martz's words, "the central, controlling intelligence" of *Paradise Lost,*[11] but his is *not* always the
centered consciousness of the narrative. That is, at any given point

11. *The Paradise Within* (New Haven, Conn.: Yale University Press, 1964),
p. 106.

in the poem, factors such as plot, action, dialogue or description will encourage readers to repress their awareness of the narrator and to transfer their identification from him to whichever character embodies the most dynamic (and compatible) consciousness in the scene. And as that may be different characters in different scenes, so too for different readers the centered consciousness can be different characters in the same scene: I identify with Satan, you with Sin.

According to Holland, "our so-called 'identification with a literary character' is actually a complicated mixture of projection and introjection, of taking in from the character certain drives and defenses that are really objectively 'out there' and of putting into him feelings that are really our own, 'in here'" (*Dynamics*, p. 278). Thus, although Milton's characters do exist "out there" in his poem, as Professor Mulder avers, prior to our reading of that poem versions of some of them existed "in here," as historical and/or literary characters whom we had previously experienced; that prior experience will not be totally repressed, a fact which Milton must have counted upon. Yet such knowledge can at least be suppressed through our willed submission to his art. As he shapes his characters according to his artistic purposes, we as readers shape them—unconsciously, for the most part—for our own psychological purposes, in effect acting as partners with John Milton. Thus, as Holland suggests, the real medium, ultimately, of an artist such as Milton "is surely the most difficult, the most intractable of all—our minds—and therefore all the greater the artist is he . . . because he creates us into creators" (*Dynamics*, p. 280).

Rather than requiring us to choose for or against his narrator then, Milton asks us to *experience* him, and to experience him in all his several roles. For like us and like the God of *Paradise Lost*, the narrator can figure forth more than one archetypal pattern. As a hero-figure in a high mimetic mode such as Milton's epic the narrator is a leader and a guide, "superior in degree to other men," but also, as the bold rider of Pegasus, he is "superior . . . to his environment," moving "in a world in which ordinary laws of nature are slightly suspended"; though identified as a human being, his actions approach the marvellous, hence there is something of

the god about him.[12] Both as guide and god, the narrator embodies the archetype of the father for those readers in his "care."
Whether this father is presenting his loving or his threatening
countenance, we as readers know him, project primal emotions
into him, and become him, introjecting his characteristics into ourselves. Historically, such projection and introjection have led most
scholar-readers to accept the narrator for reasons which have to
do not only with *Paradise Lost* as literary creation but with themselves as creators of *Paradise Lost*. Others, like Professor Mulder
and an unknowable (but probably large) number of lay readers,
reject the narrator for similar reasons. Few reactions in either
class are likely to be without ambivalence; being a father figure is
a risky proposition, as reader response to Milton's God amply
attests.

Milton's poem is, of course, notable for its father figures, and
it is to be suspected that the critical controversies which continue
to rage over Satan and Adam, for example, are only likely to be
resolved at the millenium, when all readers of *Paradise Lost* have
come to terms with their feelings about their parents and about
themselves as parents or parent surrogates (e.g., teachers). Typo-
logical study, though informative, can contribute little toward
the resolution of the problems Milton's readers have with his
characters. Understanding that Christ is a second Adam, for example, is not the kind of knowledge that can alter every reader's
accumulated *experience* of the perfection and the imperfection of
fathers. Not typology, but typology's ground of being—whether
that be the Collective Unconscious (Jung) or the Personal Unconscious (Freud)—is the region, the soil, the clime, which must
be explored in order to begin to understand the dynamics of
reader response to Milton's *dramatis personae* and to his poem as
a whole.

As Freud himself was well aware, all descriptions of mental
processes must be metaphorical: Adam's "Reason," "Fansie," and

12. Northrop Frye, *Anatomy of Criticism: Four Essays* (Princeton, N.J.: Princeton
University Press, 1957), pp. 33–34.

"mimic Fansie," with all their "joyning," "disjoyning," and "mis-joyning" (V. 100–13) are only more simplistic and less schematic than Freud's ego, id, and superego. Of greater pertinency than Milton's popularization of Renaissance psychology is the revelation of his narrator that he makes his narrative—or it is made for him—at night, either while he sleeps or while he is in that trance-like state of reduced motor and increased alpha-wave activity which precedes sleep (and esthetic activity).[13] Milton himself thought this phenomenon significant enough to allude to in three of the four invocations of his epic. Those who read Milton's narrator autobiographically tend to pass over such information as a fascinating but critically irrelevant fact. It is worth noting, however, that these three references make a distinct contribution to the development of the narrator's character, reinforcing the reader's sense of him as a special person, even a special kind of poet: not only a blind bard but perhaps a seer, a visionary. In addition, these references have generic implications, obliquely implying that *Paradise Lost* as a whole is a dream vision, thereby linking Milton to that ancient tradition generally and to Dante particularly. Finally, these references can be regarded as Milton's own contributions to the literature of creativity, constituting an implicit hypothesis about the relationship between dreams and art.

A similar if more formalized hypothesis is advanced by Freud in "Creative Writers and Day-Dreaming" where he speculates that the writer transforms dream materials, which are personal, into literature, which is public.[14] As to how this process works, Freud cannot even guess: "it is the [writer's] innermost secret." This atypical retreat from the unknown can be regarded as symptomatic of Freud's ultimate failure to work out a viable theory of creativity, as even so sympathetic a student as Lionel Trilling has observed.[15] Trilling himself has made significant contributions to

13. Colin Martindale and James Armstrong, "The Relationship of Creativity to Cortical Activation and Its Operant Control," *Journal of Genetic Psychology* 124 (June 1974):311–320.
14. See note 9 above.
15. Lionel Trilling, "Freud and Literature," in *The Liberal Imagination* (Garden City, N.Y.: Doubleday, 1953), p. 43—cited in text as *Imagination*.

the development of a critical approach to literature based upon Freudian principles, and Trilling's work has been complemented by others. The most comprehensive, plausible, and scientific of these is the one set forth by Holland in his abovementioned pioneering work, *The Dynamics of Literary Response*, and subsequently refined and improved in his *Poems in Persons* and *Five Readers Reading*.[16] A full-scale application of Holland's model to *Paradise Lost* would be far beyond the scope of this essay. Hence, what follows is merely a prolegomenon to a study of the dynamics of reader response to Milton's poem, a series of hypotheses about what seems to happen when readers read *Paradise Lost*, focusing mainly upon the narrator. Whether that is what *should* happen is a question with which more traditional Milton criticism must deal.

As we have seen, Milton's narrator implies that his narrative had its genesis in dreamlike states. It follows then that *Paradise Lost* will embody some of the qualities of dreams, though not necessarily their more obvious qualities. Ever the rational positivist, Freud was inclined to regard all literature, all art—even works of the most "realistic" character—as dreams, at least in the sense that when we respond to them we are responding not to material reality (except as ink or paint) but to "illusions." Yet, as Trilling has pointed out, this apparently pejorative view of esthetic objects, so contrary to Freud's personal veneration for artistic geniuses and their creations, is based upon a conception of reality that is simplistic even by Freud's own standards. On this point, Trilling quotes Jacques Barzun: "A good analogy between art and *dreaming* has led [Freud] to a false one between art and *sleeping*. But the difference between a work of art and a

16. See notes 1 and 10 above, and Norman N. Holland, *Poems in Persons: An Introduction to the Psychoanalysis of Literature* (New York: Norton, 1973). The most recent criticisms of Professor Holland's approach to literature have been those of David Bleich, "The Subjective Character of Critical Interpretation," *College English* 36 (March 1975):739–55, and Frederick Crews, "Reductionism and Its Discontents," *Critical Inquiry* 1 (March 1975):543–58. Professor Bleich's essay indicates certain weaknesses in the model set forth by Holland in *The Dynamics of Literary Response*—but these have been corrected in *Five Readers Reading*. Professor Crews deplores what he calls "confessional criticism," toward which, in his view, Holland's hypothesis leads him. Yet Crews does not fault Holland's model nor does he offer a clear alternative to the critic who would employ psychoanalysis in the study of literature.

dream is precisely this, that the work of art *leads us back to the outer reality by taking account of it*" (*Imagination, p.* 43).

Such discrepancies are rectified in Holland's approach, in which *Paradise Lost* would be perceived as a kind of public, controlled, esthetic "system" for stimulating private, potentially manageable dreams: a literary work, Holland claims, in effect "dreams a dream for us" (*Dynamics,* p. 75). Milton's narrator presents us with his dreams or their products (he is less than clear on this and, it would seem, deliberately so). These dreams constitute the text which the poet Milton entitles *Paradise Lost,* a book which he introduces with a fit against rhyme and for whose twelve subdivisions he composes arguments, giving the dream a frame which conventionalizes it and locates it in the realm of published literature. We approach literature, says Holland, "as we approach just about everything else in life, with a wish for pleasure. . . . No doubt we expect other things as well: information, sophistication, status, pity and fear, satisfaction of curiosity" (*Dynamics,* p. 74); but pleasure, at any or all levels ranging from the most physical to the most cerebral, is primary. The achievement of pleasure, in Holland's view, depends upon the capacity of a poem like *Paradise Lost* to enable a gratifying transaction to take place, a transaction in which "we draw upon the treasury a literary work provides to re-create our own characteristic psychological processes" (*Readers,* p. 247). Such a re-creation involves mainly unconscious selecting from among the varied materials which the work offers (as dreams involve the unconscious selection of repressed materials) in order to make up a satisfying fantasy; "however, the ego does not simply fantasize. Rather, it imagines, partly consciously, partly unconsciously, a satisfaction that balances the competing demands of the [ego, id, and superego] and the external reality of the text. That is, fantasies represent a compromise among the drives toward pleasure, the warding off of guilt and anxiety, the tendency to repeat old patterns, and the creative push to achieve new satisfaction from this new experience" (*Readers,* p. 125).

If the experience of reading *Paradise Lost,* for example, does *not* yield pleasure, it is because the reader has not been able to correlate the poem successfully with his idiosyncratic psychical personality. Such a reader either cannot accommodate Milton's epic to his characteristic patterns of response to literature and life—the poem offers him negligible ego-reinforcement—or he is unable to accommodate himself to the poem, to enlarge his perceptions of and possibilities of response to this esthetic experience. The reader, "considered as the continuing creator of variations upon an identity theme," responds to *Paradise Lost* much as he relates to life, using the poem as material with which to "re-create" himself (*Readers*, pp. 128–29).

Central, then, to the process of reading Milton's poem is the generation of characteristic unconscious fantasies—"clusters of wishes deriving from the stages in which children develop" (*Readers*, pp. 117–18)—or, in the terms of myth-criticism, archetypal actions involving figures and symbols which represent wishes and impulses to be gratified and/or fears to be experienced or allayed (*Dynamics*, p. 31). While this process would presumably be entailed in reading any literary work, from a limerick to *The Life of Samuel Johnson, L.L.D.*, reading an encyclopedic poem like *Paradise Lost* would seem to be especially conducive to it.

The poem's sheer scope and bulk, plus the fact that different fantasies characterize different readers, make it impossible here to do any more than suggest some of the kinds of fantasy likely to emerge out of the transactions between reader and text, even text particularly associated with the narrator. But since, in the course of three hundred years, a number of readers have recorded their responses for posterity, it is possible to test (if only crudely) the fantasies cataloged below against what we tend to think of as the objective criticism of Milton's poem.

One fantasy which Holland has found literature to generate with some frequency is expressive of "phallic assertiveness"— wishing for and having feelings of power, authority, and autonomy. This mental state, originating as it does with that early period of development which clinicians term "the phallic stage," is frequently balanced by fears of vulnerability. Fantasies of phallic assertiveness are characteristic not only of Milton's narrator but also, it would seem, of Milton's critics, for it is one which Holland has observed to be associated with "speech [and with] seeing, learning, or otherwise prying into things" (*Dynamics*, pp. 42–43):

Instruct me, for Thou know'st . . .

(I.19)[17]

Celestial light
Shine inward, and the *mind* through all her *powers*
Irradiate, there plant *eyes,* all mist from thence
Purge and disperse, that I may *see* and *tell*
Of things invisible to mortal *sight.*

(III.51–55)

Thou with *Eternal Wisdom* didst converse,
(VII.9)

No more of *talk* where God or Angel Guest
With Man, as with his Friend, familiar us'd
To sit indulgent, and with him partake
Rural repast, permitting him the while
Venial discourse unblam'd: I now must *change*
Those *Notes* to Tragic . . .

(IX.1–6)

Fantasies of phallic aggressiveness, according to Holland, can also be stimulated by works containing strongly assertive elements (*Dynamics,* p. 43):

That to the hight of this great *Argument*
I may *assert* Eternal Providence
And *justifie* the wayes of God to men.

(I.24–26)

Thee I revisit now with *bolder wing,*
Escap't the Stygian Pool, though long detain'd
In that obscure sojourn, while in my *flight* . . .
I *sung* of Chaos and Eternal Night . . .

(III.13–15,18)

17. In the quotations from *Paradise Lost* which follow, words and phrases potentially associative of particular fantasies have been italicized. This has necessitated omitting italicizations from the original text. Otherwise, all quotations are based upon *The Complete Poetry of John Milton,* edited by John T. Shawcross (Garden City, N.Y.: Doubleday, 1971).

                        . . . yet *argument*
        Not less but *more Heroic* then the *wrauth*
        Of *stern* Achilles on his Foe *pursu'd* . . .
                              (IX.13–15)

    Likewise associated with this fantasy-pattern are materials
involving motions of omnipotence of thought, magic, and tele-
kinesis (*Dynamics*, p. 44):

                                  I thence
        Invoke thy aid to *my adventurous Song,*
        That with no middle flight intends to soar
        Above th' Aonian Mount, while it *pursues*
        Things unattempted yet in Prose or Rime.
                              (I.12–16)

                        . . . and at the *voice*
        Of God, as with a Mantle didst *invest*
        The *rising world of waters dark and deep,*
        Won from the void and formless infinite.
                              (III.9–12)

            . . . *above* th' Olympian Hill I *soar,*
            Above the *flight* of Pegasean *wing.*
                              (VII.3–4)

                        . . . if all be mine,
        Not Hers who *brings* it nightly to my Ear.
                              (IX.46–47)

    "Closely linked to omnipotence-of-thought fantasies," Hol-
land continues, "are those of repetition," often expressed in images
of cycles and circles and associated with female figures (*Dynamics*, pp. 44–45):

        Of *Man's First* Disobedience, and the Fruit
        Of that Forbidden Tree, whose *mortal* tast

Brought Death into the World, and all our woe,
With *loss of Eden*, till one *greater Man*
Restore us, and *regain* the *blissful Seat*,
Sing Heav'nly *Muse* . . .

(I.1–6)

Taught by the heav'nly *Muse* to *venture down*
The dark *descent*, and *up to reascend* . . .

(III.19–20)

Up led by thee
Into the *Heav'n of Heav'ns* I have presumed,
An Earthlie Guest, and drawn Empyreal Air,
Thy tempring; with like saftie *guided down*
Return me to my Native Element . . .

(V̆II.12–16)

If answerable style I can obtain
Of my Celestial *Patroness,* who deignes
Her *nightly visitation* unimplor'd . . .

(IX.21–23)

As has been mentioned earlier, phallic-assertive fantasies can
have their anxiety components: seeing and learning can discover
danger (as Adam and Eve find out to their cost); aggression can
lead to counter aggression; the achievement of power and autonomy to their loss. Thus, the invocations of Milton's narrator entail materials from which readers can unconsciously generate
anxiety as well as wish fulfillment. There is, for example, the anxiety of ignorance, of not knowing:

What in me is *dark,*
Illumin, what is *low* raise and support . . .

(I.22–23)

> But *cloud* in stead, and ever-during *dark*
> *Surrounds* me, from the chearful wayes of men
> *Cut off*, and for the Book of knowledge fair
> Presented with a *Universal blanc*
> Of Natures works to mee *expung'd* and *ras'd*,
> And *wisdom* at one entrance quite *shut out*.
>   (III.45–50)

Aggressive postures such as those taken by the narrator can also bring one's physical and psychological vulnerability to consciousness:

>   ... but thou
> Revisit'st not these *eyes*, that *rowl in vain*
> To find thy piercing ray, and *find no dawn;*
> So thick a drop serene hath *quencht thir Orbs* . . .
>   (III.22–25)

> Least from this flying Steed unrein'd . . .
> *Dismounted*, on th' Aleian Field I *fall*
> *Erroneous* there to *wander* and *forlorn*.
>   (VII.17,19–20)

Fantasies of phallic aggression can also entail anxiety arising out of an apparently threatening social or natural environment:

> On *evil dayes* though *fall'n*, and *evil tongues;*
> In *darkness*, and *with dangers compast round* . . .
>   (VII.25–26)

> But drive farr off the *barbarous dissonance*
> Of *Bacchus and his revellers* . . .
>   (VIII.32–33)

> . . . unless an *age too late,* or *cold*
> *Climat,* or *Years damp* my intended wing
> *Deprest . . .*
>
> (IX.44–46)

To reiterate: the preceding citations are intended to illustrate only how some the language employed by Milton's narrator can be viewed, if not simplistically as symptom formation, at least as associable with the so-called phallic assertive fantasy. The evidence does suggest, however, that such a fantasy is a part of the identity theme of that literary character. If, following Holland's model, that identity theme correlates with those of individual readers, and if those readers also succeed in identifying with the narrator, Milton's words become capable of creating a "controlled association," in which a repressed fantasy of phallic assertion can arise in the course of reading *Paradise Lost.*

Milton's poem is, as has been implied above, "overdetermined"—replete with materials for generating the widest variety of impulses, wishes, anxieties, and their attendant fantasies. Even continuing to restrict our attention to Milton's narrator will discover other examples. There are, for instance, the narrator's notable confrontations with the sexuality of "our general Mother" and her spouse. The same stage of infantile development which gives rise to fantasies of phallic assertiveness is also the *locus* of the so-called primal scene fantasies. These fantasies of unconscious eroticism generate strong feelings of curiosity and excitement:

> . . . nor turn'd *I ween*
> Adam from his fair Spouse, nor Eve the *Rites*
> *Mysterious* of *connubial Love* refus'd . . .
>
> (IV.741–43)

but also fear and confusion, and even disgust:

> Carnal desire *enflaming,* hee on Eve
> Began to cast *lascivious* Eyes, she him
> As *wantonly* repaid; *in lust they burn* . . . .
>
> (IX.1013–15)

Psychoanalysts regard the phallic and oedipal stages of infantile development as being closely related, and so, too, are the
fantasies associated with those stages. Oedipal materials are especially characterized by emotional ambivalence; awe and love in
the face of parental power and autonomy and wishes to identify
with the possessors of such qualities are strongly felt, but so too
are fears of the threats implicit in a rivalry situation. Similar
ambivalence can be detected in Milton's narrator. His heavenly
muse is, he reminds us constantly, a female who visits him nightly
and succors him, but who can, in spite of his implorings, withold
herself from him. A heavenly born goddess, she is associated with
fecundity and creation (I.19–22), and also with an "Almightie
Father." In the invocations that father is only alluded to, never
addressed directly. The poem as a whole, however, is heavily
imbued with his power and, in addition, with the power of that
malign father Satan, whom the narrator regards with fear and
contempt but also grudging admiration. Furthermore, there is
that fallen father Adam, whom the narrator can both love and
pity. "Any work of art dealing in depth with love and hate," according to Holland, can lend itself to the generation of oedipal
fantasies (*Dynamics*, p. 46), and *Paradise Lost*, if one is to judge
from its critical canon, is no exception to that principle.

Emotionally explosive material then is a marked characteristic of Milton's poem, material which the unfit among his audience are, if we follow Holland's hypothesis, unable to manage
psychologically in terms of their individual identity themes:
"Each of us creates at least his own way of walking, talking, smiling, sitting, sleeping, loving, fighting, eating, and all the rest.
Presumably we also create our own ways of seeing films and plays
or reading poems and stories. Identity implies, too, that all these
problems have a unity, particularly that we meet and create external reality by the same strategies we use to manage internal
reality" (*Readers*, p. 113). Thus, if a reader responds positively
to *Paradise Lost*, "he has been able to put elements of the work
together so that they act out his own lifestyle." He has succeeded
in making Milton's *dramatis personae*, his plot, his diction and
rhetoric, "resonate" in harmony with his own expectancies, with
the "characteristic cluster of hopes, desires, fears, and needs" with

which each person approaches any new experience. In this way the primal emotions and unconscious fantasies arising out of the experience of reading *Paradise Lost* are "managed" so as to yield gratification, esthetic pleasure (*Readers*, pp. 113–14).

This, however, is only one of four processes which are, in Holland's conception, necessarily involved in "liking" such a work as *Paradise Lost*. The second process, for example, entails another form of "management": "If the reader has a favorable response toward a work he must have synthesized from it all or part of his characteristic structure of defense or adaptation. He must have found something in the work that does what he does to cope with needs or dangers. By 'adaptation' one ordinarily means the progressive, constructive, and maturational mastery of inner drives and outer reality. 'Defense' means a mechanism put into action automatically and unconsciously at a signal of danger from without" (*Readers*, p. 115). Unlike many literary works *Paradise Lost* offers materials for adaptation almost directly in the implied exhortations of the narrator, "Hail wedded Love, mysterious Law, true sourse / Of human ofspring" (IV.750–51), or in the exhibitions of "mastery of inner drives" by major characters, "Henceforth I learn, that to obey is best, / And love with fear the onely God" (XII.561–62). Like other complex literary works, Milton's poem offers numerous formal devices as part of its array of materials for employment in unconscious defensive strategies: its generic patterning, elements of structure and even its prosody, its connections with Christian and classical mythologies and with the literary tradition, etc. Included here as well is any formal instruction its readers have received, such as that provided by the canon of Milton criticism: "For a reader to match his defenses by means of elements in the story, he must be able to satisfy his ego with them at all levels, including his 'higher' intellectual functions. Thus, it is the matching of defenses that draws on a reader's concern with language, his experience of prior works, his critical acumen, his taste and all things people bring to bear when they deliberately evaluate literary works" (*Readers*, pp. 116–17).

The third process identified by Holland has already been alluded to above: it is that wherein "each reader uses the material he has taken in from the literary work to create a wish-fulfilling fantasy characteristic of himself" (*Readers*, p. 117). If one of those fantasies be the "phallic-assertive," he may well respond most strongly to figures like the narrator and/or Satan. If submission to the father (the "negative oedipus complex") is more characteristic of his psychical personality, he may "omit" (in the clinical sense of that term) Satan and identify mainly with Adam and/or Christ. One implication of such transactions is that "the true hero of *Paradise Lost*" can be seen as, in Freud's phrase, "His Majesty, the Ego";[18] that is, not the reader himself, not even the reader who follows the path of life set forth in Milton's poem, but the psychical personality which copes satisfactorily with Milton's text. Whether or not such a one *consciously* perceives himself as the poem's hero, the psychological process of reading it almost requires him to have hero feelings.

The fourth process involved in positive reader response to a work like Milton's poem directs attention to the question of "what *Paradise Lost* really means." As it turns out, what the poem really means may be less significant from a psychoanalytic perspective than the fact that to all favorable readers it *will* have meaning. Each reader will make sense, his own sense, of the poem:

> By means of such adaptive structures as he has been able to match in the story, he will transform the fantasy content, which he has created from the materials of the story his defenses admitted, into some literary point or theme or interpretation. In doing so, he will use "higher" ego functions, such as his interpretative skills, his literary experience, his experience of human character, in general his subtlety and sensitivity. He will bring to bear the social, moral, or political ideas that already embody congenial transformations for him. He will, finally, render the fantasy he has synthesized as an intellectual content that is characteristic—and pleasing—for him. (*Readers*, pp. 121–22)

Thus even agnostic and atheistic readers can find gratification in *Paradise Lost*, not because they necessarily have suspended their disbelief in the general statement which informs the poem, but more positively because, through their characteristic defensive

18. "Creative Writers and Day-Dreaming," *Complete Works*, p. 150.

strategies, they have been able to make a kind of sense out of the poem that can be accommodated within their identity themes: "The individual cannot work with an idea in a secondary-process way—that is, in the intellectual and aesthetic transformation [of the fantasies arising out of his interaction with the work]—unless he is in a position to inhibit any unpleasure that may proceed from it, . . . unless he can match his defenses" (*Readers,* p. 122).

If Holland's hypothesis is correct, no end to the debates about the meaning of *Paradise Lost,* its hero, or its narrator is in sight. But while such a prospect might be cause for undergraduate despair, it is not likely either to surprise or dishearten the Milton scholar. Rather it may be seen as a confirmation of the special richness of Milton's greatest poem and also of the infinite variety—perhaps even the "heroism"—of its "fit audience, though few."

5

Love Sublimated *Upon Appleton House*

James M. Kiehl

U*pon Appleton House: to my Lord Fairfax*, probably written in 1652 or 1653 when Marvell was about thirty, is a brilliant underworld-poem that explores the poet's dilemma in love. Marvell's poem is a counterpart to traditional epic of the sort attempted by his contemporary William D'Avenant, probably the ridiculed "Forrain *Architect*" in the first stanzas. It is essentially a private poem at the furthest possible remove from epic's public grandeur, yet in miniature it reflects—it literally epitomizes—the conventions of epic, which are currently recognized only imperfectly or not at all. In Marvell's time, a neoclassical era, not only was epic the zenith of poetical ambition but the counterpart or miniature epic derived from it was a flourishing genre. Milton's *Paradise Regained*, Dryden's *Absalom and Achitophel,* and both Pope's *Windsor-Forest* and *The Rape of the Lock* are various instances of the kind.

Upon Appleton House is basically founded on a most important and easily noticed epical convention: the hero's central adventure to the underworld. In epic, this otherworld is an extraordinary counterpart to our usual limited experience, and the hero there seeks the wisdom to solve his own and his society's problems. Marvell's poem presents a poet-persona who conducts us on a physical and imaginative tour into the Fairfaxes' retirement estate. Ultimately he takes us into the deepest woods, his special haunt among the birds and trees. There we discover much about the poet's own most private sensibility during an otherwise obscure period in Marvell's life. The poet's predicament exactly mimics, in a familiar domestic milieu, the epic hero's agony in the great world. The poet suffers an acute conflict of allegiances. He is secretly in love with Mary Fairfax, the prized scion of the house, who is destined to preserve the family's social integrity by an opportune, noble marriage. When the Fairfaxes retired from public life, they took Marvell along with them to Appleton House to serve as the precocious adolescent girl's tutor. And at its core the panegyric he offers on the estate hieroglyphically delineates his predicament, his reflection on it, and its resolution. Had Marvell taken Mary, of course, he would have incurred the Fairfaxes' enmity and wrath for the mesalliance, for ruining the family's prospects through her. But despite his temptations, the abduction of Isabel Thwaites as a precedent within the Fairfax genealogy, and his near rendezvous with Mary by the river (82–90), the poem concludes with the poet's entirely circumspect deference, and he leads us back to the house that will shelter him from the ominous night of his imagining.[1]

Although students of seventeenth-century literature find Upon Appleton House attractive, and though they consistently regard it as an important, though puzzling, work, their appreciations appear to be mostly intuitive. Responding skillfully to some among the poem's many handsome images, they are annoyingly arbitrary or merely opportunistic in choosing what to notice. Or if more thorough, as is Rosalie Colie in her richly eclectic and erudite essays, their attempts to define the poem's themes are disappointingly timid and too generalized.[2] But mostly, they fail to see the ninety-seven-stanza poem whole, fail to respond to its structural dynamics. Consequently, they cannot assimilate the

1. Citations of Upon Appleton House and references to it are according to H. M. Margoliouth, ed., The Poems and Letters of Andrew Marvell, 2nd ed. (Oxford: Clarendon Press, 1952). Unless otherwise noted, parenthesized numbers refer to stanzas of the poem.
2. Rosalie L. Colie, "My Ecchoing Song": Andrew Marvell's Poetry of Criticism (Princeton, N.J.: Princeton University Press, 1970).

poem; it does not inform them correctly. They may notice, for example, that the birds which the poem's poet-persona encounters in the woods are symbolical (65–70), but if they explain that the woodpecker may condemn a rottenness in the noble Fairfacian oak (68–70), they fail to specify the taint. If they explain the conventional nightingale fairly well (65), they falter on why the poet finds the stock-doves so mournful (66) or on why exactly the poet should "through the Hazles" see "The hatching *Thrastles* shining Eye" just in the moment he treads on strawberries (67). There has been no completely satisfying explanation of what the poet is doing in the woods rather than touring the house itself. To instance clearly significant critical failure to see the poem whole, one only need cite the usual inability to assimilate the lengthy historical narrative about Mary Fairfax's ancestor Isabel Thwaites (11–35). And the frequent thematic appraisal that the poem presents a traditional debating contest between reflective and active modes of life, while not utterly in error, is sadly off the mark as it imputes arid scholastic significance to an intensely personal and fascinating drama.

Too hastily attributing a particular poem to its presumed literary tradition abuses both literary history and the poem. To best make sense of a long and difficult poem, we must first discover its own coherence and design. To do otherwise jeopardizes the opportunity to discover the full resonance among its parts. To see the whole correctly depends on appreciating how all the parts function integrally. But possessing a correct intimation of the whole often resolves an ordeal with an enigmatic part. Such working from the whole, however, is the riskier and subordinate proposition. Students content to resort to the ostensibly helpful extraneous generalization may not get the poem exactly wrong, but they probably surrender gaining either the truest general understanding or much intellectual excitement. When *Upon Appleton House* is seen only as a rambling and dispassionate philosophizing on topics such as retirement and meditation and not as the underworld adventure it is, the reader misses the intriguing personal drama that vitalizes the poem's moral and ethical observations and properly makes them as memorable as and more important than any of the many images and witty figures.

Students desiring to understand *Upon Appleton House* richly and for themselves are at first likely to face a usual critical problem with a long poem. We may find it difficult to hold in our imaginations all the parts at once so that we can reflect upon each, relative to our developing and shifting sense of the whole. The solution to this problem is first to generalize our sense of the parts into a quantity mnemonically more manageable than, say, ninety-seven stanzas. Some stanzas—for example, those presenting Isabel Thwaites's abduction (11–35)—obviously group into something like complete episodes or scenes. Or we may notice that another substantial quantity of stanzas (61–81) contain the poet and us in the woods on the Fairfax estate. Then finding parallels, we see that another group of stanzas (36–46) locates us in the manor's cultivated garden and yet another takes us to the meadows and fields at some distance from the house (47–60). Persisting in this way, trying to suit our abstractions to the events or situations we find in the poem, we can divide the whole into six discrete units for the sake of memory and are prepared to try out how they pertain to each other. It is easy to see, for instance, that despite the active presence of other characters in some parts, only one character, the poet, appears substantially in more than one part. And obviously then, *Upon Appleton House* itself results from the poet's describing and praising the estate. But we further notice that his observations are somewhat ordered in space, time, and value. And so we see that the poem loosely dramatizes a generalized day during which the poet guides us on a tour through both the estate and his confidential imagination and during which we may learn more about him than about anyone or anything else.

To the Door: Decorum in House and Poem (1–10)

The poem begins with an ambiguity about whether it remarks upon the Fairfaxes' house or on itself, Marvell's poem, for "this sober Frame" is pertinent to either and refers to both. Neither house nor poem, the first stanza asserts, is made by a "Forrain *Architect*" who would deface nature to construct his art. The witty accusation is that the foreigner is not a great artist. He is not a big man but only bigheaded, and his design in grandeur is a painfully foreign, unnatural monstrosity. In all likelihood this specifically alludes to Sir William D'Avenant and to his putative epic, *Gondibert*, to which Marvell's poem later refers ironically (57). As poet laureate, D'Avenant actively supported Charles I and was knighted by him during the first Civil War. In his "Preface to *Gondibert*," he employs metaphors of a building and furnishings to refer to his own poem. And because Marvell appears to have seized from those metaphors elements with which to impugn false architecture, we are tempted to suppose that he not only commends the Fairfaxes' modest manor and his own underworld poem but that he also maligns D'Avenant's pretentious attempted epic. Whereas the false artist ravages the natural terrain, *Upon Appleton House* contrarily presents a poet who is fond of the landscape. He studies it and virtually identifies with it instead of reducing it and trying to reshape it.

The poem's second stanza solidly establishes nature as the standard of creation. It asks why man, among all the creatures, is so disorderly as to build unproportioned dwellings. The assertion that animals' "Bodies measure out their Place" directs us to the answer that a big head, which was focused on in stanza 1, makes man unruly. Man's head—his self-consciousness, cerebration, and egotism—separates him from other creatures, not necessarily to his advantage. Noticing that some men demand outsized houses, stanza 3 implies that such a man's head is empty as well as big. The dwelling only diminishes the dweller; the immense space jeopardizes him as if he were dust in the wind. And the third stanza goes on to ask a question yet more rhetorical than the question in the stanza before. It is yet more evidently its own answer: "What need of all this? . . ." No matter how casual its manner, this question about utility is a basic Renaissance test. And the stanza not only notices the puny man in his big house but also further discloses the source of the indecorum. "Marble Crust" suggests skull as well as large building, and "Mote of Dust," the brain-drifting in that skull. The stanza's last lines explain the vain man's error with immense and damning resonance. He wants to rule and manage the world rather than be at home in it, despite the scriptural myth of Babel and its fearful injunction to know one's place. Moreover, these lines also hit again at D'Avenant, whose *Gondibert* is "superfluously spread" because he deplored the traditional anthropomorphic machinery of gods employed for cosmic concentration and integration in the antique, pagan epics. He altogether banished from his own poem such machines for vertical integration and no doubt hoped instead "by Breadth the World t'unite."

Next, *Upon Appleton House* turns to admire its own topics, which are directly contrary to the foolish men and their works scorned in the prior stanzas. Like the first stanza's ambiguity in "this sober Frame," the fourth stanza's assertion that "all things are composed here" permits us to suppose that both the Fairfax manor and Marvell's poem on it are referred to. Logically, again the primary reference is to the house, as the succeeding stanza's reference to "These sacred Places" confirms. But the poem itself also still operates as a secondary referent, which we will more certainly learn when the poem carries the poet further into nature, where he seeks assimilation to the woods (71–77) and at last obediently responds to the sun's descent and nightfall.

Another of the poem's topics admired in stanza 4 is the "larger sized Men" who, in an earlier, "more sober Age," deigned to bend and fit themselves to circumstances rather than vice versa. Finding things "Like Nature" is, as in stanza 2, the principal measure of value. But again, as in stanza 1, the term "sober" possesses favorable connotation. And it appears that not *all* art is impugned. Stanza 4, like the one before it, ends with scriptural allusion that values acts of human will and self-discipline. It recalls Jesus' Sermon on the Mount and his metaphor about the wide gate and broad way to ruin, opposed to the strait gate and narrow way to heaven (Matthew 7:13–14). And the stanza may also echo another of Jesus' metaphors, about a camel passing more easily through a needle's eye than the rich man can enter heaven (Luke 18:24–25); it intimates that humility is a paradoxical attribute of true greatness. Although *Upon Appleton House* is not exactly a religious poem, it unquestionably examines and evaluates morality and ethics, as we shall more certainly infer from the poem's second major part, about Isabel Thwaites. In complement to the fourth stanza's allusion to a prior golden age, then, stanza 5 supposes the future's reverent regard for great men like Vere and Fairfax and its quandary that such big men dwelt so humbly as at Appleton House. The Romulus legend is cited as a confirming antique precedent for the great man's virtue having been molded in some significant way by his circumstance, wittily "his Bee-like Cell." Thus the poem's initial equation is complete. Appleton House is a modest dwelling for great men, to counter the absurdly big houses for small men noticed at first. The poem transforms the relatively small house, a potential embarrassment to the panegyrist's ambition, into an ethical and spiritual asset. Correlatively, Marvell's modest counterpart epic itself possesses corresponding merit.

In stanza 6, the poem explicitly celebrates humility as its capital human virtue. Humility can miraculously suit the great man to the small house or get him "through *Heavens Gate*" (4). Notably, the wonder that "Things greater are in less contain'd" is no longer exemplified by an abstract and effete scholastic puzzle. Instead, the great man is now housed in a suitably new fashion. The stanza implies that trying to bring the whole round world down to earth to fit it into the epic poem, when done in the trite old conventional ways of D'Avenant, is a tired, empty stunt like trying to square the circle. Contrarily, *Upon Appleton House* employs novel means to embody its properly focused Renaissance world, which is Man. Both "Those short but admirable Lines" and "These *holy Mathematicks*" suggest again, as do stanzas 1 and 4 before, that not only the humble house contains the great man but so do the numbers of Marvell's poem. Indeed, the poem's lines are two syllables shorter than typical English heroic pentameter. Arranged in eight-line stanzas, however, they make a Renaissance verse-form named the Square.[3] And so these stanzas are a general instance of the exquisite mimetic verses exactly tailored to their subjects everywhere in the entire poem. By em-

3. John M. Wallace, *Destiny His Choice: The Loyalism of Andrew Marvell* (Cambridge: Cambridge University Press, 1968), pp. 237–238.

ploying his own more familiar devices and homely stratagems Marvell more nearly achieves traditional epic goals than does D'Avenant. By focusing his unpretentious poem on Appleton House he invents a microcosm, a united and ordered miniature world, that opens out to embrace the macrocosm, as the poem's shifts in scale and perspective repeatedly suggest. Corroboratively, the next stanza asserts that both house and poem strain somewhat to contain "the *Master* great" (7). In a note, Margoliouth suggests that the description notices the domed cupola over the hall at Appleton House as it stood in Marvell's time. But beyond that, the stanza's fantastic illusion that "the swelling Hall / Stirs, and the *Square* grows *Spherical*" bulging in response to the great man's presence is a promising figure for greater energy and excitement than occurs in sleepy imitations of epic. And since the house is figured as distressed and as scarcely containing the great man, it may be worth noticing that Fairfax himself is not at all a persona in the poem.

In several tight aphorisms the first couplets of stanza 8 summarize the relation between dweller and dwelling examined in all the poem's early stanzas. The aphoristic manner lends rhetorical dignity, a quasi-moral superiority, to the great man's situations in a modest house and in a tutor's poem. Certainly the master is greater than his house, and yet the house itself is also admired in the stanza's second half. The poem in this regard only imitates the great man's own taste, for the preceding stanza (7) apprises us that the modest situation pleases him. Functional simplicity, or utility, is especially remarked as the house's merit, and we recall the conclusive utilitarian test with which the foreign architect's unproportioned building is dismissed in stanza 3. Stanza 9, then, goes on to specify the great man's uses of the modest house, and they are ethically noble. The front door is open in welcome. The rooms are daily filled with friends. The lovely trope that the house's "*Furniture*" is "*Friends*" raises the house above ordinary consideration, despite the apparent explanation that it is mostly ornamental and only a momentary stopping place for its master. The expressions "*Mark of Grace*" and "Its *Lord*," moreover, turn our attention toward religious significances and away from commonplace meanings. Here, as in stanzas 4 and 5 before, the poem seems to attribute unusual piety to the great man and virtually sacred use to his house. Margoliouth cites Fairfax's own verses, which regard Appleton House as a worldly stop on his soul's progress to Eternity.

The house is consistently also Marvell's poem. The poem is based on the house as the house is built upon "the Place." Thus the poem also functions in ways corresponding to the house. It no doubt entertains "Its *Lord* a while," but more important, it is also only a verbal marker for the actual experiences it represents. Like the *"Frontispice"* to the house, the artifact of the poem is only an "open Door" to the "Rooms within." Paradoxically, this particular poem's referents, its "Rooms within," are exclusively outside the literal house. Appositely, the last architectural feature here in the poem's introductory first part is the doorway to the house. And as we go into this house—that is, this poem— in the entire remainder of the poem, we do not literally enter the house but are instead led to the grounds, and perhaps the world, beyond. Nor do we enter the poem. That is, the poem hereafter significantly ceases to be its own topic in any remarkable way.

The poem's entire first part effectively ends with stanza 10, which insists the distinction of Appleton House among all the Fairfax residences is that it belongs to "Nature." Implicitly, Appleton House more truly expresses its master's spirit than do his other more conventionally suitable houses. By association, the poem again, as in stanza 4, seems to establish nature as the base of its positive values. The gardens, woods, meadows, and floods cited as distinguishing the manor are precisely the kinds of landscape that order the poem's imaginative progress. Rather than taking us into the house itself, the poem turns us to its situation in the landscape, in nature. Only at the poem's end when night falls and the situation looks alien does the poet turn us back toward the house. The poem does something like reverse our usual senses of inside and outside. We might ordinarily expect the inside, the place of art and society, to be the focus of our interest. But *Upon Appleton House* instead offers us the outside as a truer inside, for it is the poet's own retiring place for imaginative activity and for his most intense experience.

ISABEL THWAITES: ABDUCTION FROM THE NUNNERY (11–35)

Although not formally signalled, the poem's second part begins in stanza 11. As we start to tour the landscape we are immediately diverted to examine the manor's history, which begins by imputing perversion to the nunnery originally established on the site. The scandalous paradox about the house that "A *Nunnery* first gave it birth" is a sardonic accusation immediately reinforced by the succeeding image of "*Virgin Buildings*" delivering offspring. Having learned to appreciate an apposite relationship between house and master at the poem's beginning, we are conditioned to suppose that houses express their residents. The physical building is not the only or even the truest sense of *the house*. And so our scandalized first impression endures, although the stanza's last lines offer a local correction that the broken-down original buildings furnished stone for the later house Marvell knew. And certainly the succeeding twenty-four stanzas portraying the nuns' perfidy in traducing the heiress, Isabel Thwaites, from her lawful, and perhaps natural, obligations aggrandize and justify our initial sense of scandal. The Isabel Thwaites legend, apart fromMarvell's possible private uses for it, perhaps admirably suited the Fairfax family's sense of its origin as it so conveniently epitomizes the English religious reformation for which Marvell's employer, Sir Thomas Fairfax, spent his whole active life.

Stanza 12 sets the scene in which the nuns elaborately seduce Isabel (13–25). But primarily it discloses their principal motive in seducing her; they are venal and covet her wealth. Not only is she "blooming" to redress their "gloomy" situation, but more measurably she is "an Heir / Which might Deformity make fair." The nuns' motive matches the venalities and other perversions of value for which original Protestants indicted the Roman Church. The stanza goes on to describe how the "*Suttle Nunns*" approach the innocent girl and reminds us of the serpent in Genesis. One nun "weav'd" words as if setting a snare for the heiress. Artfully this nun expresses "Thoughts long conceiv'd." The term "conceiv'd" sustains the sexual innuendo aimed at the nunnery in the prior stanza. The nuns are portrayed as thoroughly deceitful adversaries to innocence. Marvell's syntax, which inserts a perfectly calculated but apparently casual parenthesis, "(As 'twere by Chance)," deftly mimics and characterizes their fraudulence.

In stanza 13 the nun's actual speech to Isabel begins by reversing the usual meaning of imprisonment. Sophistically she argues that the nunnery liberates the nuns, does not confine them. She contends that the cloister preserves the innocents within from the savage world and beastly men outside. Whatever its effect on the girl, however, the nun's sophistry (Marvell's dramatization) is too full of walls, hedge, bars, gates, locks, and grates to fool us. Her speech in the following stanza (14) is also strangely contradictory. She describes the nuns as both the pagan sort of Amazon warriors and also waiting brides according to the Christian parable that authorizes cloisteral life (Matthew 25:1–13). Although parallel in form, these descriptions disagree in substance and spirit. The nun is confusing, if not confused, about her sexual identity. But more important, either her seduction speech is perniciously unethical or her values amoral, for this whole stanza, and especially the last couplets, intimates a substantial theme of self-indulgent sensuality (incense, perfume, cosmetic) that is sustained and intensified through her entire appeal to the girl. After referring to tears in cloister, the nun in stanza 15 is quick—too quick—to assure the girl that the inmates weep only for joy in their own pleasures or possibly in pity of her, because she is without their pleasures within. The nun alleges that in the nunnery they suffer no griefs, that each nun is both *"Spouse"* and *"Queen,"* that they are doubly fortunate, that they are assured of places in heaven, that they have it good both ways. But essentially, if not literally, the conditions *"Spouse"*—meaning one who is promised, contingent, or dependent—and *"Queen"*—a sovereign, a ruler—conflict as did the figures Amazon and bride in the preceding stanza. Closely examined, the nun's assurances are not perfectly sound. Then more certainly, in the stanza's last line she exposes her venality by her special regard for "brighter Robes and Crowns of Gold" as her heavenly rewards.

During her address to Isabel the nun has gradually raised her subject from its beginning onus, the commonly unattractive condition of cloisteral seclusion. Now in stanza 16 she can more affirmatively describe cloisteral life as realizing and fulfilling the scriptural ideal for a triumphant life. She describes the nuns' typical devotions and lessons, and their embroidering sacred vestments. Her description relates their embroidering holy legends—especially saints' faces—onto altar clothes to their endeavoring to make over their own lives in the image of the saints. Essentially, the nun pictures a life of art in the nunnery. Embroidering vestments is art in body; disciplining and shaping lives is art in spirit. Then in the next stanza (17) the nun first dares overtly to invite the girl to take their vow and enter the order. But in doing so, the nun egregiously flatters Isabel that her face would serve the nuns as a palpable model for their embroidery of the saint. By this shocking, heretical inversion of the correct relationship she herself has just described (16), the nun almost certainly subverts any possibility that her words are legitimate, that she can be trusted. In the stanza's last lines the nun bribes Isabel by proffering that her face will be published through the world in the guise of the saint on altar clothes. This sleazy attempt to excite vanity and lust for fame utterly contravenes the presumed cloisteral ambitions of humility and anonymity.

But the daring nun goes further in proposing that Isabel is destined for a higher place than to wed William Fairfax to whom she is betrothed (18). The nun pretends religious zeal in her invitation to the girl. But the lubricious wit of Marvell's couplet " 'Twere Sacrilege a Man t'admit / To holy things, for *Heaven* fit" attributes a virtually wanton depravity to the nun and indicates that the fire she claims to feel is not pious zeal but sexual desire. In the stanza's last lines she commits flagrant sacrilege as she fulsomely foresees Isabel becoming a saint. The nun's flattery culminates by asserting that Isabel's "Beauty" consecrates her (19), but the nun's professed high regard for her is wholly sensual, not spiritual. Having artfully raised a high estimate of the girl's worth and destiny, the nun proceeds to find young Fairfax beneath Isabel. The subtle nun vilely insinuates that Isabel's marriage would be tantamount to her disdaining heaven and would preclude her heavenly destiny. And so the nun advises the adolescent virgin to accept young Fairfax only as an idealizing devotee rather than as a real lover. That Isabel deserves a worshiper, not a mate, is her counsel.

After disposing of Isabel's betrothed, the nun next proceeds to sketch a prospect of the girl's life in the order (20). She offers the girl both love and obedience, saying that each nun will be both sister and servant to her. But like the nun's contradictory descriptions, such as the Amazons who are brides (14) and the spouses queens (15), this promise is also implictly faulty. Moreover, the succeeding offer to alter the rules of the order to suit Isabel's pleasure implies outright perversion of the cloisteral purpose. The corrupt nun's next inducement offers the girl sovereignty over the whole nunnery. Isabel is promised she will become superior in the order when the aged abbess soon dies. Ironically, again the nun's compliment "How soft the yoke on us would lye, / Might such fair Hands as yours it tye!" much more exposes her own corrupt motives and character than does it characterize the girl she tries to flatter and bribe. Marvell's verse is immensely rich; in such circumstances the yoke on them would indeed be a lie. Again, as before (17 and 18), the temptress brings her fulsome flattery to a crescendo when she suggests Isabel will work miracles and possibly become a saint (21). The nun, of course, should know that this bribe she offers is blasphemous. Above all else she should recognize the error in presuming sanctity, in trying to command God's grace. Marvell's ingenious verse makes this climax in the seductress' address subtly ambivalent and self-damning. Her cleverness exposes her. Out of the nun's mouth "Those Virtues to us all so dear" refers to sensual pleasure, wealth, fame, and power that we have learned she loves more than the orthodox religious virtues. Sanctifying such "Virtues" as are dear to her is only a wantonly ignorant revaluing of depravities. Such sins, "once sprung," increase fast indeed, as we see mimicked in the instance of the nun's own character being quickly exposed when at last she gains an opportunity to express in words "Thoughts long conceiv'd" (12). The only perfection to which she can be led is perfect depravity. The only miracles worked by such sanctity as she possesses are *miracles* of vice. And the three stanzas remaining in the nun's seduction speech are in fact wantonly salacious.

In stanza 22 the nun offers the girl a life generous in pleasures apart from its putative piety. Considering its source and context the nun's casual assurance that the promised pleasures are not vices exactly belies itself. Her assurance is so unwittingly ambiguous and ironic that we readily assent that the nuns do not banish their delights as vices and that their order is not "so nice." The nun's smooth figure for the cloister's sweet delights, however, is founded on fruit-preserving and is designed, no doubt, to seem homely, innocent, and wholesome. Her metaphor confusingly identifies either the nuns' piety or their pleasures as a preservative against the decay of the other, the fruit. But if piety is the fruit and pleasure the sugar, the nun's piety is incomprehensibly perishable. It is certainly at odds with any orthodox meaning of piety if pleasures are necessary to preserving it. If on the other hand pleasure is the fruit and piety the sugar that preserves it, the nuns abuse their religion. They exploit a more worthy means to a less worthy end; they commit sacrilege. And yet more certainly damning to her metaphor and the sensibility that contrived it is the nun's perhaps unwitting allusion to the scriptural legend of Eve's sin. In this context the nun ironically seems happy to propose preserving and savoring ruinous sin. Such "Arts," as in the next stanza (23) the nun names these cloisteral activities, are inimical to the nature of piety.

These arts then slide further into indecency as the nun boasts that in the nunnery they handle "Natures finest Parts" (23). Again, as before in stanza 18, the possible sexual euphemism renders her expression salacious, perhaps inadvertently. The succeeding lines in stanza 23 catalog the cloistered nuns' tastes (seeming to satisfy sensual appetites for decor, costume, cosmetics, drugs, and delectables) in a descent from flowers for dressing altars, to amber and balms, and down into the sink of pastes "as Baits for curious tasts." This catalog passes from upright and natural experiences into potentially dark arts as if the nuns might actually be witches as young Fairfax angrily alleges (26) and as the poet also regards them (34). The stanza's final couplet intimates how far from piety the nuns may be sunk. The temptress' coy query "What need is here of Man? unless / These as sweet Sins we should confess" teasingly suggests that covertly the nuns may even enjoy sexual license despite their vows. The insinuation's furtiveness exactly dramatizes that the nuns also probably pervert even the rite of confession to unrepentantly discharge their guilts. But then in the following stanza (24) the seductress openly offers sexual license as a bait for curious tastes and as if without moral or spiritual liability. Again, as in stanza 14, the nun recurs to the scriptural parable about constant vigil, but she salaciously travesties it and completely besmirches the ideal of cloisteral life it symbolizes. The temptress finishes her seduction with the transparent satanic assurance that a trial of the proffer is perfectly safe (25).

In the latter half of stanza 25 the poem turns to record how the family ancestor, young William Fairfax, responded to displacement from his betrothal. Ostensibly he was jilted for piety and religion, but actually he was cheated by the nuns' lubricious proselytizing capsulized in the stanza's last line, which reports about the traduced girl Isabel: "The *Nuns* smooth Tongue has suckt her in." The succeeding stanza (26) presents young Fairfax, who knows the fraud and tries in vain to enlighten the girl. By complaint to Isabel, in this and the next two stanzas, he tries to alert her that she is betrayed by the nuns' ingratiating art of persuasion. The young man possesses no similar art to counter theirs, however, and he quickly lapses into futile invective. Nevertheless, his hyperbole that the nuns are "Hypocrite Witches" who have reached beyond their walls to enchant Isabel and steal her from him is basically just. Frustrated that their cloister has failed to debar them from cheating himself and Isabel, he threatens death to them. And we may notice that in a way—but with reversed value—his bitter complaint confirms the subtle nun's boast in stanza 13 that the cloister does not imprison the inmates.

Angrily, young Fairfax denounces the nunnery as a thorough fraud: "vice infects the very Wall" (27). With a contemptuous pun on "alter" he charges that the nuns unnaturally corrupt everything about them just as they have perverted their rites and their own natures. He already has ample reason to believe that Isabel's innocence cannot possibly survive proximity to them. He holds them so effectively vicious that he is sure they affect even the stone with which the nunnery is built, else it would

come down on their heads as nature's vengeance on their corrupting arts. Obviously he believes the institution deserves the
ruin in fact brought upon it by the Reformation's dissolving
religious orders and seizing their properties in the next generation
after him. And the next stanza (28) has him prophesy that such
an evil establishment cannot last long. His prediction functions
just as prophecies often do in epic, where the epic poet's knowledge of his culture's past history functions in his poem to fulfill
his antique characters' prophecies about their future. This whole
device for dramatic irony authorizes that the prophet, in this
instance young Fairfax, possesses marvelous prescience, wisdom,
and integrity. Middle couplets in the stanza have Fairfax disclose
his mysterious knowledge of the nuns' presumably secret depravities. And having ourselves witnessed the nun's lurid invitations,
as in stanza 24, we are privileged to recognize that his allegations
are just. Somehow he has seen their vices and knows the nuns
want not Isabel but her wealth. And by what we learned in
stanza 12, this indictment also seems confirmed. Foreseeing the
order's fall, Fairfax finally pleads with Isabel that she flee from
the "Ruine." Fairfax's word "Ruine" resonates Marvell's very
occasion for offering this entire episode in the family's history
(11). All the dramatic irony convinces us of the youth's integrity
so that as his speech to Isabel ends we believe his care for her
is as sincere and wholesome as the subtle nun's was fraudulent
and malign.

Next the poem summarizes young Fairfax's predicament as
his sensibility is divided between the claims of "Religion" and
"Right" (29). His religion seems opposed to his desire to rescue
Isabel, but his sense of right, which he learned from religion in
the first place, exonerates his desire. And because his religion in
teaching him right did not overawe and confuse his understanding but cleared it, we infer that his own clear sight is at
last the adequate arbiter of the conflict he suffers. Thus neatly
capsulized we have the Protestant position in the great religious
conflict at the Renaissance. In subsequent stanzas young Fairfax's
breaking into the nunnery to save Isabel virtually symbolizes the
acts of Reformation in England. The last couplets in stanza 29
restate Fairfax's dilemma; he is caught between his courageous,

soldierly impulses to act in his own right on one side and stric-
tures of moral and ethical law on the other. And we admire his
honor as his passions are checked by his allegiance to the law
and justice. He is a just man. It is his breeding, his heritage.

The poem goes on to represent that young Fairfax knows a
mere physical assault against the nunnery would yield him a poor
triumph (30). And so, epitomizing English Reformation, he gets
legal sanction from the Crown to prevent his unfairly losing
Isabel. The nuns nevertheless still resist his legally buttressed
"Right," and the stanza ends with the poem's ominous question—actually a terrible warning—to the nuns: "do you know /
Whom you resist? . . ." The local answer is awful enough. They
deny the Crown and its putative Divine Right. The more comprehensive answer, which we learned in the prior stanza (29), should
be terrible to them. They resist "Religion" and God. And perhaps
most impressive to us, in another time and place and maybe with
other values, they defy history. The next stanza (31) answers
the momentous question with a resounding heroic prophecy
trumpeted in yet another rhetorical question. By our knowing
the characters' futures and the history of the Reformation we are
privileged to know that the nuns are awfully wrong. They defy
the Fairfaxes' historical destiny as an entire race of English warriors. But the whole prophecy, actually a history, implies that
they defy God to whom they presumably owe all allegiance.
For—Fairfax or not—it is certainly God's offspring who "Shall
fight through all the *Universe*," and messianically conquer Britain.
They defy "Fate," if we appreciate that epithet from epic antiq-
uity. The poor nuns presume to interfere with the history of
God's world and especially the English Reformation to which the
Fairfaxes and Marvell were deeply committed. And so, instead
of the supposed bride's being ready to receive the son of God,
their bridegroom, when he comes, as they should according to
their cloisteral model (14), we see them act unnaturally as
Amazons to oppose young Fairfax's assault on the nunnery.

With acute irony, the whole assault, presented in stanzas 32
and 33, is nevertheless appropriately figured as a sexual entry. It
is exquisitely burlesque in manner. And if there is, in fact, little
honor in it, as Fairfax supposed (30), Marvell's earlier defense

of the modest house and of his own poem again seems applicable in exculpating Fairfax:

> So Honour better Lowness bears,
> Then That unwonted Greatness wears.
> Height with a certain Grace does bend,
> But low Things clownishly ascend. (8)

Without insisting on the nuns' presumptuous phallicism in pushing "*Wooden Saints*" and "*Holy-Water Brush*" into "the Breach against their Foes," their defensive weapons—including their "Chain-shot" rosaries, their cannon-loud lungs, and their sharp tongues—are ridiculously impotent and futile. Like many images and figures in Marvell those in this entire burlesque conflict especially resemble familiar figures in Milton. The nuns' cannon, for example, much resemble Satanic devices in Milton's burlesque war in heaven. And the first line in stanza 33 not only presents the nuns as finally ineffective but conclusively imputes evil to them; they are likened to flies. The rest of the stanza, with compelling sexual figures, pictures Fairfax penetrating the cloister wall and entering the nunnery's "unfrequented Vault." He exposes its superstitions, its frauds, and its illicit wealth. His opening the secrets to clear view epitomizes the Protestant redress to the Church's frauds. And penetrating all the way to the altar he finds Isabel among the jewels there. Figured in this way, their meeting is the sexual union that will beget the English Reformation the nuns would prevent.

The following stanza (34) pictures Fairfax, like a prince in romance, rescuing Isabel, the princess, away from her enchantment. Instantly, as Fairfax seizes Isabel, the nuns' spell is broken, and they are left moaning and wailing in confusion as if they are at last exposed as the gypsies or witches they were alleged to be (26). The way that the nunnery in one moment is "dispossest," as if by magic, mimics the sudden way the Crown, later in that century, by fiat dissolved monastic orders and seized their properties. Stanza 34 goes on to sustain the simile of this more-than-century-old episode in Fairfax genealogy as an antique, childhood romance or fairytale. This patently artificial close to the story helps us notice the story's symbolic function within the poet's whole work of art. As a denoument, the following stanza explains that when the Crown dissolved religious orders the nunnery-lands reverted to Fairfax possession because of William's marriage to Isabel (35). The legalism "by Escheat" recalls the nun's "cheat" alleged by Fairfax (26) and seems to imply that the Fairfaxes gained possession as a redress for the cheat he suffered. It is poetic justice. The stanza and the poem's entire second part then end with an encomium on the Fairfaxes. It occurs in the terse ironic reversal that only since ceasing to be a nunnery has the property's intended sacred destiny as a *"Religious House"* been fulfilled.

This second part of the poem on the abduction of Isabel Thwaites to establish the Fairfax family line resonates throughout the whole poem in various ways, but several of its functions within the poem are especially important. By an elegant correspondence and displacement, it presents—in the marriage-exploit of William Fairfax, the ancestor—a loose paradigm of the active military career of Marvell's employer, Sir Thomas Fairfax, the supreme Parliamentary general in the Civil Wars, before he retired to Appleton House to behave as described in the poem's next major part. Additionally, the Isabel Thwaites legend offers certain correspondences to the situation of Sir Thomas' daughter Mary, whose own betrothal and marriage are anticipated late in the poem. But most important, the legend offers the poet himself precedent and guidance in resolving the conflict of allegiances he suffers as he lives in the Fairfax family at Appleton House.

The Soldier's Garden (36–46)

The third major part of *Upon Appleton House* starts at stanza 36. Here the poem turns our attention from the historical digression in part two back to a tour of the premises, which began and was interrupted in stanza 11. After our virtual night-journey, in part two, to visit the legendary ancestors struggling in a dark time, we in effect are raised from bed in the morning to meet the new day during which we will be led through the estate and into our guide's sensibilities. Part three, then, is located in the cultivated garden close about the house itself, and it especially examines the possibly puzzling, untimely retirement of Sir Thomas, the great general. Stanza 36 itself is transitional. It is half historical, like part two, and it is half about the manor's garden, the scene of part three. It celebrates Sir Thomas' forebear and namesake, also a soldier, who, in the preceding century retired to Appleton House and playfully designed his garden as mimic fortifications, an act that inevitably reminds modern readers of Sterne's My Uncle Toby. But the poem does not distinguish much between the ancestors who planted the garden that endured to Marvell's time and the poem's current Sir Thomas, who is as properly designated "Heroe," who has also retired to Appleton House, and who might himself have come "From that blest Bed" to walk in his garden on this very morning that the poem locates us there. In fact, Marvell's poem compresses and fuses all the Fairfax warriors, and especially William Fairfax of part two, into a figure of the great general.

At stanza 37 the poem responds to and sustains the trope invented by the garden's founder. Here and in succeeding stanzas of part three the garden is presented in delightfully innocent mock-heroic figures that culminate in the favorite traditional figure of England itself as the post-lapsarian world's paradisal garden (41). Stanza 37 describes the dawn sky as a great flag and the bees in the garden as parading sentinels. Colorful blossoms are identified with military ensigns. Flowers are personified as soldiers roused to arm themselves, with munitions of fragrances, for the day's drill. The succeeding stanza (38) pictures flowers firing fragrant vollies in salute to their "Governour," Sir Thomas, and his wife as they pass by. The flowers do not similarly recognize the daughter Mary, however, for they think her a flower like themselves. And not quite rebuking the flowers for their inadvertent compliment, the poet adjudges them correct except that she is sweeter and fairer than they. At the dramatic climax to the entire poem, when in the last part Mary passes by and transfixes him on the wooded river bank at dusk, the enlightened poet will foremost recognize and praise her himself (82–93). But in stanza 39 the poet primarily salutes the flowers in compliment to their color and odor. Here the poem is keenly witty in having the poet relay or translate the flowers' "shrill" and echoing salutes in sight and smell to his own exuberantly sounded words of praise. And we are reminded that the ancestor originally designed the garden-fort to aim for all the human senses (36). The latter half of stanza 39, still in mock-heroic figures, admires the good discipline and orderliness in the retired soldier's formal garden. This appreciation of art in what might be nature's place alerts us that this garden is near some middle in the poem's whole progress that starts us in the artificial situations of house and history then advances us outward through garden and cultivated fields finally to arrive at more exclusively natural woods and river.

Stanza 40, although still offering mock-heroic flowers and bees in a sweetly innocent garden, essentially turns part three away from the microcosmic enclosed garden and toward the macrocosmic public world. This substantial turning in part three anticipates a similar turning at the poem's stunning end and is signalled by the stanza's showing the garden's appearance at the turn from daylight and colors to night. The turning is also significantly indicated by the gorgeous cosmological figure of stars wheeling through the heavens, circling the pole in stately order. The daytime's sentinel bees now give way to the stars, seen as superior sentries who stand watch and patrol by night. And the shift in scale of the figures, from bees beneath to stars overhead, signals a shift of great thematic magnitude. It is just like such effects in Milton at his metaphysical best, in the Nativity Ode and in *Paradise Lost*. Thus after idyllic scenes of Fairfacian innocence, stanza 41 macrocosmically starts a lament for war-torn England's evil plight. England as a ruined "Garden of the World" is a dark counterpart to the little garden in good order at Appleton House. Alluding to scriptural legend, the stanza addresses to the nation an epic question: "What luckless Apple did we tast, / To make us Mortal, and Thee Wast?" According to scriptural and cultural typologies widely promulgated by contemporary religiosity, England is figured as the Garden of Eden (and correlatively as Israel, as in stanzas 49 and 51), now after the wars fallen to ruin. Important correspondences emerge in the poem when stanza 41 apostrophizes England to evoke its traditional sense of sheltered insularity. As England was formerly a sanctuary from the world and its troubles, Appleton House is a sanctuary from contemporary national strife. As England once was a paradise, Appleton House still is. England's ideal state as the Promised Land is now all contracted to Appleton House. Exactly consonant with its epic precedents, Marvell's counterpart, miniature epic establishes its subject at the center of the world.

Succeeding stanzas (42 and 43) further develop the lament for the nation's ruin. Clever comparisons between gardening and military experience go on as before but with the terms reversed and with a sorrowful tone opposite the playful mock-heroic before employed to present the garden at Appleton House. England's Civil Wars have so overrun the erstwhile garden that pleasant sport of the sort Fairfax's ancestor enjoyed in making his garden remind him of his triumphant foreign campaigns (36) is only a fond memory that renders the present grim situation an even more bitter spectacle. Once the nation was entirely filled with gardens, "But War all this doth overgrow: / We Ord'nance Plant and Powder sow" (43). Within the nation, only Appleton House, it appears, by its symbolically still flourishing garden, is a last bastion of the innocent past. Then the poem's lament for the nation gives way in stanza 44 to conjecture that Sir Thomas Fairfax might have restored England's garden. This proposition of course flatters Marvell's employer, and from what we know about contemporary events, it is unlikely that he could have succeeded in what the more capable Cromwell failed to accomplish. But the conjecture is not absurd. At his retirement, Fairfax was still nominally Cromwell's superior in the army and his political ally, and might plausibly have shared in the Protectorate to rule England. Instead, however, he somewhat mysteriously relinquished his military career and public life alluded to in the last couplets in stanza 44 and retired to Appleton House to cultivate the garden of his spirit. He might have been very high and powerful, but he chose the homely way of humble self-abnegation.

The next stanza (45) implies that Fairfax's withdrawal from public life, power, and celebrity is a sober self-discipline to prepare him for death and eternity. Retired to his country manor he allegorically gardens his spirit to weed out *"Ambition"* and to cultivate *"Conscience,"* a rare heavenly plant with prickly leaves "But Flowrs eternal, and divine. . . ." These figures suggest that his modest house itself intimates his piety (4 and 5) and indicates his serious regard for his eternal life beyond residence at any of his worldly properties (9). He seems to have retired to practice stooping to get "through *Heavens Gate*" (4). Thus we find that part three in the poem resonates with part two. Like his forebear William Fairfax, Sir Thomas too has had to choose between apparently conflicting allegiances and, electing to retire from his service in the supposedly religious wars, has, like his ancestor, again made his manor a *"Religious House"* (35). Stanza 46, the last in part three, conclusively establishes that in his retirement Fairfax's vision is aimed beyond worldly conflicts and concerns. Were he disposed to continue the wars in which he had so distinguished himself, the Adversary is possibly within close range. Prelatical property is temptingly close to Appleton House. Actually, however, the inimical Archbishop is long gone from his castle. Nevertheless, almost as if to incite Fairfax to renewed engagement, the stanza compares the great General's perhaps typical act of gazing out over the landscape from his home, to military acts of aiming emplaced artillery. The beams of his vision are likened to ballistic trajectories. But the general fails to emulate the Archbishop's political ambition. This last echo of the prior mock-heroic manner indicates by its feeble endurance that the retired soldier can no longer be rallied to the old conflicts. Instead, the last lines in part three assert that his attention "plays" innocently over the meadows to which the poem will take us in part four. And by its indefinite syntax the stanza's last sentence intimates that behind his wandering or vacant eyes the great mans' inner or spiritual vision probably sees some distant prospect beyond the world. We recall that at Appleton House he cultivates "Flowrs eternal, and divine, / That in the Crowns of Saints do shine" (45).

To the Abyss through the Meadows (47–60)

The poem's fourth major part, which starts at stanza 47, is immediately striking. In the very first line the poet himself first appears explicitly as an actor in the poem's scenes. And he remains the principal persona through the poem's entire second half, playing a larger role even than Mary. This is remarkable, if not puzzling, in a poem presumably upon his employer's estate. But here at the poem's structural middle the poet seems to take over from Sir Thomas as if to follow in the direction of that pious man's gaze (46) toward outlying places of spiritual or imaginative life and away from more immediate, common worldly concerns. And in fact, in the poem's second half the poet sustains the unexpected direction the poem took earlier (10 and 11), and he goes yet much farther afield from the house. Having toured the carefully designed, decorative gardens in the poem's third part, in the remainder of the poem he passes through functionally cultivated meadows to at last enter the dense natural woods and arrive at the river, the definition of which is variable and vague because of its fluidity, floods, transparencies, and reflections. Altogether, the poet appears to make a progress, by stages, from scenes of art to nature. And as he proceeds toward the meadows and other outlying property in the poem's latter half, he calls that landscape an "Abbyss" (47), a name from antique cosmologies to designate the otherworld, the uncharted metaphysical expanse beyond the known world and counterpart to it. Corroboratively, stanzas 47, 48, and 49 immediately liken the meadows beneath Appleton House (46) to an ocean and reinforce our inference that the poet here at the poem's middle leads us to a fluid otherworld that may unsettle our accustomed certainties.

As the poet leads us down into the meadow a paradox of scale astonishes us. We are removed from our familiar human advantage of standing superior to the landscape and looking out over the meadow stretching below. And instead of being distantly amused, as we may once have been, that people down below in those meadows appeared—from our perspective—miniscule and insect-like, we are ourselves plunged into the deep meadow grasses and made to see them close up. The grass now towers tall over us so that the grasshoppers riding high on the stalks can look down and patronize us. Both *Paradise Lost* and *Gulliver's Travels* contain inversions like this, with similar meanings. The reversal implies that from another vantage point or to another sensibility than our own we might appear as insignificant as either insects or distant people usually appear to us. That the grasshopper could in some sense seem to us like a scornful giant may shake our usual presumptions about who or what we are, but it certainly apprises us that we are passing into a region strange and obscure to us. The following stanza (48) speculates that human interlopers might easily become lost in the meadows' alien depths. It supposes they will be righted and come up safely, however, if their adventure is justified—as gravity aims the mariner's lead—by a pure and worthy purpose such as gathering flowers. They rise alive by bringing back something valuable. To successfully negotiate the otherworld we will have to be steadfast in purpose and may have to relearn fundamental values according to our experience there.

In stanza 49 the poet marvels that the meadows at Appleton House frequently change according to sun and season. But he introduces a traditional metaphor to regard the meadows as a theater of elaborately staged and wonderfully shifting scenes. And whether the poem is actually composed in harvest-time or not, the poet nevertheless visualizes mowers come to harvest the ripe grass. Typically now in the poem's second half we more clearly see that the poet's actions and imagination control his circumstances as much as vice versa. It is the poet's mind in which the tableaux at Appleton House are staged. This is yet clearer as the river is in later stanzas raised to flood the meadow (59) and then lowered again (79) as if all in the same day. And we begin to suspect that the poem's truest otherworld lies within the mind of the poet, who started obviously imagining scenes in the consistently artificial mock-heroic garden in part three.

In stanza 49 the poet shows us mowers passing through deep grass as if they were scriptural Israelites parting the Red Sea. Such figures were endemic to contemporary Puritan imaginations, which commonly resorted to scriptural analogues—their own underworld, as it were—to establish superiority of their doctrine by its prior, sacred authority. Furthermore, the mowers look like antique warriors as with vigor and enthusiasm they mock-heroically "Massacre" the grass (50). The hyperbole might be absurd except that it possibly alerts us to our precarious human situation. And we more surely recognize our own vulnerability when one of the mowers inadvertently kills a young bird nested in the grass. He abhors killing the innocent bird, for he possesses morality—not merely superstition—based on an appreciation of decorum. Contrary to the nuns who defied William Fairfax, the Crown, and God (31), he fears "Fate." Like an authentic antique hero or perhaps even a modern general with conscience (45), he senses his relationship and responsibility to the rest of his world. He is a reverant harvester.

Contrarily, the servant girl who carries refreshment to the mowers in the fields feels no such compunction at all (51). Opportunistically, she snatches up the dead bird to carry it away for her supper. Then, excitedly, she seizes yet another bird to increase her meal, and by extending the allusion (Exodus 14–16) she wittily—perhaps impertinently—improves the poet's scriptural analogue (49). As a food bringer and devourer, she, like the mower, shares in the universal food-chain, but she fails to appreciate its meaning that relates food to killing and to her own eventual death. We might even notice that appositely the bird she seizes to eat is female and that moreover the poet likens the brash girl herself to a hawk. Strangely, this impertinent girl furnishes quasi-objective evidence that the poet is himself an actor present in the scenes the poem observes and records. And her own small act of wit—and of poesy, too—may at last implicate even the poet himself in the awful food-chain, as in a sense he feeds his imagination and art on the events of their lives. We should suspect that these stanzas implicitly explore and explain, among other things, the General's motive for withdrawal from the wars that otherwise appear to exonerate his cause and demand no retirement. Is the ambition he wished to weed (45) not like the servant girl's ignorant greed; is the conscience he tilled not like the unlucky mower's scruple?

The first couplets in stanza 52 aphoristically lament the

slaughtered birds and confirm that they emblematize widespread
human suffering in the Civil Wars. The poet's apostrophe "Un-
happy Birds!" may well be an address to all the common folk vic-
timized in the strife: the mower who has remorsefully killed by
accident and the foolish girl who compounds the evil by wantonly
exploiting it and, in effect, killing again. The stanza's last lines
poignantly dramatize the compounded horrors of war. It kills and
kills again. It ruins posterity, as pathetic "Orphan Parents" indicate. Thus stanza 53 advises innocent birds to somehow get out
of the way, for "The Mower now commands the Field." This counterpart epic again describes harvesting as warfare as if responding to traditional epic, in which war is typically described as harvest. Pertinently it is exactly Fairfax's retirement from public life
and the wars that permits us alternative scenes disclosing what
warfare means. Earlier, the poem seemed to regret his retirement
(44–46), but now we see that he may have been first to recognize
dire consequences of his own and the nation's military adventures.
Perhaps his retirement is itself an endeavor to answer the poem's
implicit question about how to restore England's once-healthy
garden (41–42).

The next picture in the series of harvesting tableaux shows
the flushed and fragrant harvesters exuberantly dancing when
they have finished their work (54). This heady celebration is described by allusion and grand epithets that implicitly compare it
to the traditional epics' representations of triumphal, heroic games
to savor life after its jeopardy in war. The dancers' concluding
sweet kiss seems to recompense their labor undertaken to renour-
ish life. Nevertheless, the succeeding, final stanza on the harvesting shows the haycocks in a sequence of sobering similes: as river-
rocks that may break boats, as pyramid-tombs rising upon the
desert sand, or as funeral pyres in military camps (55). These
figures give us a last look at war's consequences, and with incre-
mental certainty they apprise us that war means ruin and death
as much as it means victorious success and continued life. No
wonder then that a great soldier might retire from such experience to be reflective and reverent about its ambivalence.

At stanza 56 the poem again theatrically invokes machines to
change scenes at will. In this more subjective second half of the

poem where the poet ranges away from the house and toward greater privacy, he again indulges his license imaginatively to abridge and speed up time (49). Thus the poem can immediately picture the meadow completely emptied after the harvest. And the poet is ready for a new start in composing scenes. As if the terrain itself were his medium rather than his topic, he first imagines the bare landscape like a blank canvas as if he were a painter. Next he regards the landscape as the new and empty world, as if he were the Creator. Finally he prefers comparing it to an empty Spanish bullring before the bulls enter for the contest. Thus in close succession we have alternative comparisons for the empty meadow, but as if the poet were only trying to choose among them, they are much briefer than the sustained mock-heroic harvest that goes before. And so we seem to come closer than before to dispensing with the verbal medium and to nearly sharing immediately in the poet's train of imagination. This effect especially suits the poem's second half where, generally, we are privileged to approach more closely to the poet as he seems gradually to draw away from others. But as free and fluid as is his imagining in this stanza, we should remark that it is not merely arbitrary; notably it is yet dependent on objective nature. And strange as it may at first seem that he finally prefers the artificial foreign arena for his comparison, the bullring is a more immediately suitable figure than the others, for he seems naturally obliged somehow to describe cows grazing in the stubble-field.

The following stanza (57) pictures the neighboring villagers turning out cattle to graze in the meadow after harvest. Then it recalls that D'Avenant's abortive epic verbally presented a disdainful painting in which God's creation of man filled the new world with mere cattle, and it wryly notices that D'Avenant, of course, must himself be among the herd for which he feels contempt. But more than further belittling the "Forrain *Architect*" (1), the stanza's principal effect is either to suppress and diminish the landscape or to raise the point of view far up above it. We notice that now the fields belong to levellers, commoners, and cattle that chew the fields flatter yet. Were it not so egregiously anachronistic we might liken the principal effects in the poem's new scene (56–58) to cinematic craning or zooming. The poet's imaginative virtuosity here rivals similar effects in Milton's great epic and is requisite in traditional epic. It is precisely for ignorant failure to achieve these verse decorums, these enriching correspondences of topic, manner, and theme, that Marvell ridicules both D'Avenant's presumption and his flat, empty poem. In the bullring, would the poet be matador and D'Avenant the bull?

Stanza 58 goes on to describe the cattle in the stubble-field as they appear from above and at great distance. The scene is first likened to the framed miniaturization of it we might see refracted on the eyepiece-lens of a telescope, not by holding the instrument to the eye in usual fashion but by holding it at some distance from the eye to objectify the image at the lens. The second couplet in the stanza asserts that, thus miniaturized in the meadow, the cattle look like spots on faces, and in fact the meadow was before described as a face (56). Clearly, the stanza's topic is vision and how shifts in point of view alter appearances and values. And as the third couplet compares cattle, which look like spots on faces, to insects, we seem returned to where we started in part four. There the poet, from up above, surveyed the meadow below, "Where Men like Grashoppers appear" (47). The third couplet asserts that to be seen adequately such miniscule objects as the spots must be looked at under a microscope that exaggerates or lies about their actual size from the usual human vantage point. But of course the spots are actually cattle seen at a great distance. By the stanza's permutations, the cattle are first small in a distant small field, next small in a close large field, then large in a close small field, and finally either large or small in a distant large field. As a result, these interacting fluctuations in both scale and perspective erode our sense of either actual sizes or distances. And about the cattle at last compared to constellations in the sky we can scarcely judge whether they are big or little, near or far. We become relativists skeptical about any supposed reality. This stanza is extreme in the metaphysical manner. Its rapid succession of interacting comparisons greatly confuse us about the difference between real and ideal or between natural and artificial. For the coy poet this fast play among images may be "pleasant Acts" (59), but for us who must follow and keep up they are dizzying and nearly disabling. We sense ourselves certainly in the

abyss he promised (47). We are consequently more than ready
for the coming change signalled, as before in the poem (40), by
an image of slow steady celestial turning in the stanza's last lines.

The flood that changes and renews the scene in the meadow
is welcome to us (59). As before (49 and 56), the poet again
abridges time, and he shows us the meadow, now inundated by
the River Denton flowing near it, at a somewhat later season after
harvest. With some punning on "Sea" and "seem'd" directly after
the perplexing stanza on perceptual relativity, the new scene
represents the flooded meadow as a sea and the cows, trying to
graze and wading in it, as islands. Furthermore, the stanza per-
sonifies the flood waters—the river become a sea—as having risen
up to invite Lord Fairfax, the erstwhile maritime commander
(44), to abandon his retirement and return to duty. Mythopoeic-
ally, their flood is indeed evidence that the waters have become
unruly without their former governor. The paradox that the flood
relieves our distress at the poet's confusing play with scale and
perspective, at his virtual flood of comparisons, is like the river
that "in it self is drown'd" and may be like the justice of finding
D'Avenant in his own herd (57). By the poet's art, nature is represented as redressing our grievance about the poet's artifice that
confuses our usual sense of nature's stability. The smooth, easy
correction astonishes us as much as the flood surprises the cows.

The last stanza in part four then disclaims further interest in
the flood scene and the verbal paradoxes it inspires (60). The
poet seems overwhelmed by the creatures in the flood and quits
them. But in parting he leaves a flood of riddles that need resolving to right a world gone topsy turvy, as in children's tales, for
reasons that are at once both natural and artificial. The world
is in fact upset by the flooded river, but the poet's witty words
describing the disorder make it more clearly appear so. Fortunately we already know the single answer to all the riddles and
can easily resolve the paradoxes that the no longer amused poet
abandons to others, to us. In this way, part four ends by compen-
sating us for having suffered the confusing shifts of scale and perspective in prior stanzas (56 and 58). The flood, which might have
been disastrous, is relief to us because it permits us to understand,
or to suppose that we understand, whereas we scarcely did before.

Of course we understand as we do, more because the poet cleverly fits his riddles to our answer than that we find an answer to his riddles. Either way, however, we somewhat regain confidence and are encouraged to trust the poet and to follow him farther into the abyss.

Altogether, part four, with its succession of scenes in the meadow, is not so apparently coherent as are the poem's other major parts. Its comprehensive theme is elusive until we look beyond its topics, ideas, or images to its manner—actually its succession of manners. First, the mowing scene appears neoclassical. It occurs as a little drama in sustained mock-heroic comparisons—a romance mode. It is not much less smoothly consistent than the similar manner for describing the garden in part three. Next, the distant prospect of cattle grazing is in the earlier metaphysical manner. Its peculiarly associative play with images is intellectually provocative, but it thwarts easy rationale and certain comprehension. Finally, the flood occurs as a primitive myth and as riddles that children might respond to. The general shift in the poetic manner of part four from beginning to end implies that the poet's underworld adventure is also a journey backward through the historical evolution in poetic styles toward the source of the art. A look beyond part four, in either direction, sustains the sense of stylistic regression we find within. Looking to the poem's beginning, beyond the fairly modern mock-heroic descriptions for the formal garden in part three, we find narrative chronicle in part two and precisely illustrated polemic in part one. Thus toward the poem's beginning we find language used for increasingly discursive, obvious referential, and public purposes. Or looking in the other direction, toward the poem's end, in part five we shall find further regression an explicit topic, although we shall not see it in the manner. We shall see the poet present himself learning birdsong and nature's sign language and generally endeavoring to become more like a bird or tree. Finally, part six will show us the poet dumb in Mary's presence as if she were a goddess whose coming marvelously stills the world. The poet there seems arrived at the preverbal—perhaps even preconceptual—source of his language. Perhaps there, at the absolute source, he is inspired by his muse. The poetic regression outlined here as a major pattern in the poet's underworld adventure exactly coincides with the poem's more general movement from art, at its beginning, to nature, toward its end. Thus in addition to its coincidental regression of historical or sociological images—from agriculture, to animal herding, to fishing in the flood—the special contribution by part four is that its modulations most concisely dramatize and signal the poem's whole movement from art to nature.

NATURE'S LANGUAGE IN THE WOODS (61–81)

Part five begins with the poet-persona himself entering the woods on the estate (61), just as part four started at the poem's middle with his descent into "the Abbyss" (47). Thus he ventures further into private experience, deeper into his underworld. And in "retiring from the Flood" he corresponds to his employer, Sir Thomas, whom the poem described as forsaking maritime concerns to retire to Appleton House (44). Wittily naming the woods his "Ark," he regards them as sanctuary from the flood and might as plausibly suppose himself a sort of Noah—"the first Carpenter," the first artist—as suppose himself among the animals. But instead, by his "imbark" pun, he seems almost to identify himself with the timber. Later stanzas, in fact, embellish this suggestion (71–77). And the poet's strange wish to achieve union with the woods purposely makes part five, which appositely contains "*Natures mystick Book*" (73), the poem's most enigmatic part.

In stanza 62 the poet describes his sanctuary as a thick "double Wood of ancient Stocks." These woods explicitly signify the two families, Fairfax and Vere, interlocked in marriage and thus intimate to us the poet's motive in coming there and wishing to be assimilated to them (76–78). The stanza's second half alleges that the united families share the whole round of life and endure eternally. By the images wittily married, both trees and people in a sense overcome death ("though many fell in War") not by magic so much as because they are prolific generation after generation and never die out, although individuals fall, of course.

Next the poet describes the entire woods, seen from the outside and at a distance, as looking impenetrable (63). His modifier "first" and especially his metonym "Eye" recall prior puzzles in visual relativity (58), and we appreciate that the woods look that way because of his particular point of view. How they look shows us where he is. Again, we meet the fact so important to this entire poem: we know about him by what he relates to. And what he sees immediately is the woods—that is, the Fairfax family—looking marvelously titanic. Looking as if they hedge in "the Night," they might be an immense primordial ark containing the eternal otherworld. It is, of course, a mythological figure for the Fairfax family tree that sends shoots (scions) "to Heaven" (62).

Stanza 64 presents the prior perspectives precisely reversed, and we infer that the poet is now within the woods and seeing it close up, where it seems relatively open and spacious. Recalling the tenor of the family-tree metaphor, the Fairfaxes known only at a distance may seem a tightly knit and exclusive family but regarded more closely may be accessible. In any case, the grand-architecture metaphors, with which the stanza continues, recall that the poem began by praising Appleton House not as extravagant architecture but as a modest, natural house, the construction of which did not demolish forests. And so it is likely that the poet regards the ancient woods, more than the modest building, as the truest family seat. Corroboratively, his architectural metaphors render the woods a temple or church nave—before, the woods were an "Ark" (61)—and in yet another sense we see the manor as the *"Religious House"* it became when the corrupt religious order was dispossessed and the property reverted to the Fairfaxes (35).

The nightingale, the bird first noticed among "the winged Quires" in this natural sanctuary, traditionally symbolizes sorrow specifically, but more generally in poetry the nightingale is the parody symbol, that is, it symbolizes symbolization and also lyric poetry. Its appearance first among the birds in the sanctuary is a sure index that they are all emblematic (65). The half dozen or so succeeding stanzas then present a succession of birds that challenge us to augur them, to interpret their significance, somewhat as the mower foresees his own fate in the rail he destroys (50).

Here the poem is so consistently emblematic that it is virtual allegory. Mysteriously, the poet is talking to us in strange tongues. And listening to the nightingale in stanza 65 are the shrubs and trees in the woods. To establish the woods as more surely symbolizing the Fairfaxes, they are boldly, even ingeniously, personified; for example, "listning Elders prick the Ear." And the family of warriors is suitably represented by such trees, for these personifications resonate with the tradition in ancient epic that compares its heroic warriors to great trees: some upright as the soaring fir, others magisterial as the strong oak, some earthshakingly fallen.

The stock-doves in stanza 66 are as clearly emblematic as the nightingale. They are love birds "whose fair necks are grac'd / With Nuptial Rings their Ensigns chast." And it is to them especially that the poet himself responds; notably he employs the first-person pronoun for only the third time in the poem (see 47 and 61). Although the nightingale is conventionally regarded as the sweetest singer of the saddest song, the poet finds the doves' song yet more poignant. And the stanza ends with both a riddle and a lament about them: "O why should such a Couple mourn, / That in so equal Flames do burn!"

The nightingale's song is aptly sad, considering the horror story of the ancient Philomela-Procne legend, which is its traditional etiology. But the poet's riddle that the doves to him sing an even sadder song can only have as its answer that their love is somehow thwarted. And so we come to suspect that *Upon Appleton House* is a veiled love-poem. If young Marvell, gone into retirement with the Fairfaxes to tutor their daughter, Mary, has fallen in love with her, then the enigma of this most challenging part five in the poem has its eminently sensible answer. Then we can more richly and readily appreciate why the poet peculiarly wishes to unite with these woods, to this house and family. And then the poet finds the doves' song sadder than the nightingale's for either of two possible reasons. The doves may foreshow to him Mary legally wed to another when he feels she should be his. And he finds their song "Sadder, yet more pleasing" because for lingering love of him she too regrets her *mariage de convenance*. Or maybe more simply, the doves signify to him his own ideal union with

her, which can never be realized because he, the commoner, cannot possess and wed her, of noble birth, without terrific mesalliance, without ruining the Fairfaxes' posterity and social destiny.
Mary was Anne's and Sir Thomas' only surviving child. Marvell
might have taken her from the house and its destiny for her (93–
94), but only with impossible ignorance or villainous ingratitude.
For though he might seem to have precedent for such an abduction in the family legend of William Fairfax seizing Isabel
Thwaites, actually the situations, despite appearances, are not
essentially correspondent. Marvell must have recognized this and
have behaved with great circumspection. He withdrew to haunt
the woods and bury his predicament in emblem, allegory, and
riddle. He sublimated his love into this poem itself. And despite
this poetic expression of his—and possibly, Mary's—burning
secret, Marvell discreetly managed to keep it from all except those
of us, three hundred years later, who are most curiously interested
not in Appleton House and its great family, as would be his contemporaries, but in his poem and in Marvell himself.

In the difficult and intensely allegorical stanza immediately
following the stanza on the doves, the poet probably augurs the
likely result should he actually pursue his desire and possess
Mary (67). The strawberries he carelessly tramples are a traditional religious symbol of both innocence and righteousness and
may figure both Mary's chastity and the family's trust in his integrity as her tutor. He is doing something like looking into their
future; the hazel is the poets' tree, Graves informs us.[4] Were
Marvell to abuse the Fairfaxes' trust and take Mary to wife, he
can see prospect of his and Mary's offspring. But in the stanza's
last half the other birds and trees may foreshow him the further
probability that the Fairfaxes would abandon even their prized
daughter were she to disgrace them. If, in fact, this stanza presents the poet's speculation about his possible future, its relative
opacity—"The hatching *Thrastles* shining Eye" only glints
through densely tangled brush—suits it. And we eke out its meaning as much by its context as by any certainty about its own
figures.

4. Robert Graves, *The White Goddess: A Historical Grammar of Poetic Myth,*
2nd ed. (New York: Vintage Books, 1958).

Contrarily, the poet's allegory about his first experiences in this woodland sanctuary, which represents the otherworld of his private sensibilities, comes to an end with greatest clarity in the three stanzas that follow (68–70). The hewel or woodpecker is traditionally a doomsday bird or judgment bird. And the poet sees it indeed testing the trees for their soundness. Reading here in *"Natures mystick Book"* (73) the poet can scarcely mistake the meaning, nor can we. Starting in stanza 68, the personification of the woodpecker as a woodsman caring for the woods is developed deliberately and at length. Stanza 69 shows that when the woodpecker finds a hollow tree he cuts into its rottenness and destroys what little is left of the tree to make it "his building." The construction metaphor recalls the architecture, with which the entire poem began, and its lesson in decorum: nature inevitably brings all things to their just proportions. Thus, even the greatest tree if become corrupt is certainly doomed to ruin. The stanza illustrates that the judgment bird can bring down even the mighty oak. And easily this allegory makes good sense. Because the noble oak signifies the Fairfaxes in this poem (93), their house is pointedly not exempt from the natural law. A hollowness in it will bring it to ruin; the principle is the same as that with which the poem began (3). Part two dramatizes the nunnery as suffering just such a fate. But the Fairfaxes' house, all through our acquaintance with it thus far in the poem, is sound and without taint. Its future, however, primarily depends on Mary's fate, and probably on her suitable marriage (93).

Stanza 70 continues the allegory by which the poet covertly explores the contingent prospective destiny of Appleton House. The oak, it asserts, is not vulnerable unless it has harbored and nourished a *"Traitor-worm,"* and by the conservative principle of original sin, if it breeds a traitor it deserves to. But the worm-eaten tree's fall completes a circle of justice, for the tree's ruin at last exposes the worm to be devoured in its turn. The worm is justly punished for its subversion. Curiously, moreover, the treachery is in a sense its own punishment. The interpretation is easy. The poet himself—Marvell, who has been taken into the house and trusted to tutor Mary—is the traitor were he to carry her off. But should he do so, the Fairfaxes would have been at fault for trusting him in their midst. This paradigm of mutual dependency and natural justice, by which error is its own punishment and virtue its own reward, recalls the mowers' food-chain that implicates the devourers in the fate of what they devour (50–53). This is the ethical core of the entire poem, as may be indicated by the poet's naming himself a *"Philosopher"* in the adjacent stanza (71). And the ethics matches that in *Paradise Lost* and in the whole epic tradition. Thus despite elaborate, veiled reflection about abducting Mary, the poet never does so, not exactly because he chooses not to but because he cannot do so, as we discover in their encounter in the poem's last major part.

The succeeding stanza (71) utterly dispels any further doubt that the entire first half of part five is allegorical and that it investigates the poet's own situation and speculates on his prospects. He explicitly asserts that the birds and trees instruct him. Further, he claims virtual identity with them just as, in various ways, he has also achieved either parity or identity with other members or elements of the manor: the mowers (51); the Fairfaxes, generally (53–54); the General, particularly (45 and 61); and perhaps cattle (58–59) and insects, too (47). Except for wings, he himself is one among the birds he visits and portrays. Turn him around or upside down and find that he is himself a sort of tree. Conversely, invert the tree and find the man; that is, interpret the emblems in his allegory and find that they refer to the poet himself.

The poet goes on to claim relation to birds especially (72). He insists that he begins to call in their language and feels sure he communicates with them, for he sees them in response transfixed on their perches in the trees. We can suppose that to amuse himself in the woods he may play at birdcalls with some success. Or perhaps the entire picture is a trope to express the poet's growing confidence in his craft. But the last lines in the stanza best indicate his situation and condition. For if the birds are transfixed in their attention to him as he tries to call to them, his concentration and intensity in observing them or any leaf on the tree is trancelike. By yet another instance of the whole poem's insistence upon circumstantial relativity, the poet portrays himself so intensely focused upon bird and branch that he is nearly drawn out of himself and transported. He is so deeply entranced, so rapt in the woods that beyond mere philosophy, he achieves foresight and prophecy (73). That is, his natural vision translates into some experience nearly supernatural, into divination and wisdom. For he is able in such moments to assimilate his natural vision of the patterns in feathers and twigs and leaves to his abstract bookish learning, his artificial vision. He is able to marry his otherworld to his ordinary world, his outside to his inside. Here in nature his experience achieves integrity and wholeness, and it satisfies the ruling premise established when the poem first appreciated the fit proportions of the house itself (4). This stanza that identifies experience in prophecy with learning in history—that integrates foresight with hindsight—conforms to the major structural principles in epic: the start *in medias res,* the concentric shape, and the precise symmetries. And as epic is the supreme, encyclopedic kind in poetry it most richly expresses wisdom about human experience. Marvell's counterpart epic, then, assures us that the challenging emblems the poet offers us in part five are not merely his private fancies but are figures of both art and nature in their mutual integrity. To conceal his predicament in love he expresses his earnest thought and feeling in artful figures that more perfectly—if cryptically—disclose his dilemma to its finest nuance.

As a witty confirmation of the wisdom he divines in the birds and woods, the poet finds leaves and other woodsy debris clinging to him (74). Such covering suggests that he is suited to the woods in which he took refuge and which seem ready to assimilate him. He is amused to remark that he has acquired a costume appropriate to the woods he imagined church-like (64). He teases us that he is nature's priest. Next he pictures himself recumbent and resting at ease in the woods (75). He appears relaxed from the intense emblematic stanzas that preceded. No doubt they severely taxed his wits as they have tried ours. And he devotes the last couplets in stanza 75 to thanking the personified woodland elements for their soothing ministrations now that his coinciding spiritual, philosophical, and imaginative crises have passed. The poet feels his mind weary, and he thanks cool breezes that clear the "Chaff," the cluttering, burdensome thoughts, from his head. The pleasant release and ease that come to him in the several stanzas since he has read *"Natures mystick Book"* indicate that he has found his vocation. At last he appears to know how to behave according to his nature.

In stanza 76 he congratulates himself that he has in these woods secured himself from assault on his "Heart" by "Beauty." Mary is, of course, the only "Beauty" in the poem who threatens such an encroachment (87). And his encounters and deep reflections in the woods seem to have rescued him from what he has come to recognize as his inappropriate desire. Thus, as will her parents when Mary eventually weds (93), he in effect also wishes to make his destiny his choice. And he is deeply glad at last to be secure, under his allegorical cover, from others' possibly resentful and damaging charges that he has had designs on Mary: "How safe, methinks, and strong, behind / These Trees have I incamp'd my Mind."

In the final stanzas on himself in the woods (77–78), he pleads with vines and brambles to permanently imprison him in the sanctuary, to virtually martyr him. The extravagant bondage figures indicate his substantial anxiety to be secured both from desire for the girl herself and from ruinous accusations. Apparently, he truly relishes becoming nature's priest. His own situation corresponds remarkably to Isabel Thwaites's situation in the nunnery before her abduction by William Fairfax and may intimate what her condition and sentiments must have been but about which the legend, as the poem presents it, is strangely silent. Why, apart from some utterly ambiguous tears (33), is her sensibility never represented? Why, for that matter, is Anne Vere —Sir Thomas' wife, Mary's mother—not an active presence in the poem (38)? And why, then, does the entire poem culminate in the poet's encounter with Mary only to have them pass at a distance in awful silent regard for one another? Are these women, across their sexual boundary from the poet, the ultimate and absolute otherworld to his experience and never to be penetrated and discovered by him?

His desire for bondage to the woods, however, is ambiguous in its implications. On one hand, he prays to be bound to his commitment to priesthood in nature that so enlightens and transports him. On the other hand, he wishes to be bound there so that his concealment endures and he not be dismissed for suspicions that he desires Mary. Furthermore, in either of these instances, his prayer is additionally ambiguous. If he wishes to stay in the woods to be secure in priesthood, does he not betray apprehension that he might again stray after Mary? Or, if he wishes to stay there to preclude anyone's knowing he has desired her, does he wish to stay there because he still desires her? In stanza 78 the priest prays for discipline. That is, the poet directs that he be chained, morning and night, to the woods, but in several locations. Each situation is significant. In the morning of his vocation, at the start of his behavior and experience, he will be placed where he is compelled to see the narrow path of wisdom and piety in his situation among the Fairfaxes, where he might stray into error. His comparing the lane between the two woods to Ariadne's thread through the labyrinth reinforces the idea. His design is not unlike Sir Thomas' own in choosing to reside modestly at Appleton House. In the evening of his experience he will be located where he must remember the flood and his inevitable judgment. There he may behold with pleasure the rightness and beauty in having studied and discovered his correct behavior. The last stanzas in part five picture him at such ease by the river (79–81). Or contrarily, he may be like one of the cattle that grazed there when the meadow flooded (59). Perhaps he will require bondage because he fears his bestial nature. He may at last prove to be a minotaur, which unless securely fettered will jeopardize the innocent girl that may wander there (82).

With the poet's directive for his placement at evening, the poem's scene shifts away from the woods and back into the meadow, where the river has receded (79). The meadow now appears more vividly colored and fresher than before the flooding, when it was exhausted by harvesting and grazing. It is like the ancient Biblical world purged and renewed and with no serpent any more—or scarcely any—to pervert it. Here at evening the poet is gratified to see the cleansed world that emerges, after his study in the woods and his commitment to his vocation. The meadow is fresher, of course, because he is, and the river is scarcely a serpent because the poet who sees it harbors no duplicity, at least consciously. In the following stanza, he directs us to look upon the

muddied river with its reflecting surface which so perfectly mirrors its vicinity that the experience of looking into it confuses the
perceiver about what is substantial and what is only image, about
what exists in the shared, objective world and what exists in the
shadowy underworld (80). The fanciful illustration that has even
the declining sun long for its reflected fellow is a witty anticipation—as if a motivation—of the sun's imminent descent. It will
seem to go to meet its mate below the horizon. But the supreme
example of the mirroring that mates perceiver and object perceived, that integrates inside and outside, that unites art and nature, that perfectly assimilates the poet to Appleton House, is the
poet's almost perfectly ambiguous and fluid description showing
his own union with the river (81). To end part five, he both pictures himself lolling perfectly at ease, perhaps fishing, by the
stream and—by exactly the same images and syntax—also per-
sonifies the river exactly reflecting—a trope for each image—the
postures in which the poet concurrently plays on the river bank.
This mirror union is utterly exquisite even to the perfectly witty
extent that both his fishing lines and the limber branches of the
willow that supports him also tie the river to him or him to the
river and sustain his prior wish for bondage.

MARY FAIRFAX, THE POEM'S SOURCE AND END (82–97)

The poem's sixth and last major part, presided over by a glorious
sunset, starts at exactly the moment the artful and playful poem
most perfectly unites to nature, the poet pictured playing. His
transporting play and his union is interrupted at its consummation
by the arrival of Mary (82), whom we scarcely glimpsed before
as a flower in the garden (38). Does this interruption at exactly
the poet's most fluid relation to the place suggest that his fishing
has in fact succeeded wonderfully? Has he designed to be located
here not just consciously to secure himself to his priesthood commitment but also unconsciously to catch a "Beauty" (76), that is,

to waylay Mary alone in her evening walk? Now, his meeting with her appears to have been the destiny of his whole day and adventure in the poem. And as the commitment he seemed to learn from birds in the woods has not yet endured a suitable test, his prayer to be tied to that wisdom may betray a just apprehension. Now, as Mary draws close to him, the suddenly self-conscious poet undertakes to adjust himself in an instant from his relaxed, natural youthfulness to manliness as if such an alteration were within his control and only requires his willing it. In stanza 83 the poet notices that "loose Nature" responds to Mary's coming and "it self doth recollect" after the preceding fluidities he discovered and shared in the woods. Certainly, at least, we ourselves see the poet in her presence recollect himself into his more socialized, self-conscious, conventional, and objective persona. Correlatively, he exercises his art on the occasion to contrive a substantial metaphor that etiologically attributes the magnificent natural sunset to the sun's circumspect deference to her. Thus the poet portrays a conventional lush sunset like those that occur in heroic literature. In his art he recollects himself from his earlier figurative novelties into traditionally more recognizable poetry.

As a precise symmetrical counterpart to the sun—above both the poet and Mary—descending, the next stanza (84) brings forth shadows—from under the banks beneath them—to veil the river and further sustain the picture of nightfall for the poem's conclusion. The hush and stillness that is commonly believed to come at dusk the poem attributes to a "modest *Halcyon*" that momentarily transfixes nature. Supernaturally, its passage suspends all activity in the world, except its own calm flight. By correspondence, Mary herself is unmistakably the halcyon bird. Here, she no longer appears as a moaning love-bird (66). When she quietly passes by—apparently never addressing the poet— she is pictured as a primordial figure that divides and rules the cosmos. Her stunning presence now really tests the poet's imagined relationship with her. Now his earlier passion is indeed transformed, as in the woods he discovered it should be, to a higher love that inspires the paean to Mary, which fills this last part of the poem and furnishes its triumphant tone. And so the poem describes the exact moment she passes by as one in which the entire natural world to its nebulous extremities becomes marvelously transfixed:

> The viscous Air, wheres'ere She fly,
> Follows and sucks her Azure dy;
> The gellying Stream compacts below,
> If it might fix her shadow so;
> The stupid Fishes hang, as plain
> As *Flies* in *Chrystal* overt'ane.   (85)

No doubt we recall the similar miracle at the moment of Christ's birth in Milton's Nativity Ode. The last lines in Marvell's stanza suggest, as the plausible explanation for the apparent miracle, that the effect occurs within the human onlooker's sensibility: "And Men the silent *Scene* assist, / Charm'd with the *Saphir-winged Mist*." This identical phenomenon occurred before for the poet when, in the woods, he so raptly focused on the birds that he was transported and they consequently appeared transfixed (72). Thus as Mary moves through the scene the poet's entire attention is absorbed by her presence, the moment is richly expanded in his consciousness, and his perception of all else but her is suspended.

Mary first appears walking near him (82). Then he sees her as the halcyon flying through the twilight landscape (84–85). Now at last she appears to him as rushing through the world more impressively than a newborn comet or a dying star, for these are ephemera but she in her passage seems eternal (86). Perhaps she appears to be a flaming angel, at the zenith of her appearance. Her passage near him, while it is sustained in the poem, incrementally excites him until he regards her motion as so fiery that for him its furious heat fuses all nature to a moment of glassy eternal perfection. His sensibilities heighten to a paroxysm, and she seems to fix nature as a great mirror that reflects her own virtues. The succeeding stanza asserts that the beauties and virtues in the elements at Appleton House—in the gardens, meadow, woods, and river we have been lead to admire—are all derived from Mary (87). And what the poem asserts is in one sense, at least, highly plausible even though our more distant regard may see it as hyperbolic. For it is not surprising that the poet himself is greatly pleased with the estate because Mary dwells in it and it is hers. If this is the love poem we have supposed it, that Mary is the poet's goddess and, to him, the source of all goodness is not astonishing.

As Mary is believed to supply the estate its beauty, the estate is reciprocally dramatized offering itself to her in return (88). The complementary composition of the response suggests that Mary is, consonant with her namesake, an improved Eve in another paradisal garden. Probably because her passage through the estate has "wholly *vitrifi'd*" nature (86), all of her natural vicinity—not just the "limpid Brook"—has become a responding mirror to serve her beauty. Even the woods serve her "higher Beauties" (89) by concealing her more mundane beauties. As a pleasant trope the woods—earlier emblematizing the family pedigree and tradition (62–63)—screen her from the world's view just as the family has in fact guarded her from the world (91). But her evening walk at the edge of woods, meadow, and river also saves her in a way, despite that it exposes her to the desires of the poet, who seems to await her there as if to compel a clandestine meeting. Her silently passing him there tests his piety and proves his resolve—discovered among the emblem-birds in the family woods (65–76)—not to try traducing her from her proper social destiny. Ironically, as the woods which taught him his correct disposition are really hers, he spares her not so much as she saves him. He owes his own correct and decent behavior to her family, her estate, and her own halcyon-like bearing there.

Nobler than to be vain of her natural beauties (we are not sure Isabel Thwaites was likewise—17 and 19), Mary is described as regarding her accomplishment in languages—her learning, her art—as her true beauty (89). And further, the poem describes her accomplishments by distributing the properties of language in tiers that ascend in value from noise, up to wisdom, and finally to piety. Correspondingly, the stanza's latter couplets build syntactically to mimic the tiers' rising. Mary's aspiration in language is, of course, represented as the highest. In this she matches the poet himself, for the poem has earlier presented him learning a language among the birds in the woods and rising on identical tiers, from sounds to wisdom and piety (72–74). This stanza that analyzes language solves for us a major puzzle about Mary's behavior. The principal drama in this last part of the poem, and perhaps the crisis to the entire poem's drama, is Mary's coming to walk by the river at evening perhaps to encounter there her possible lover. Yet the poem dramatizes her as only passing nearby her tutor and never addressing him. This is peculiar behavior for one presumably so accomplished in languages, unless, as stanza 89 implies, not all language occurs by noise. In the poem's earlier fifth part where the poet describes himself in the woods and conversing with birds in the branches he believes that when his sounded language is utterly spent he nevertheless continues his rapt communion by signs that the birds divine. Commonly or objectively the reverse is, of course, more true. That is, beyond hearing the birds' calls, the poet at last reads their "Signs"—their plumage, for example (73, 66), or their postures and actions (67–69). But his intense focus on them has, to his sense, also inverted the relation so that the birds understand him as well as he understands them. Thus in his final dramatic encounter with Mary, the halcyon bird, her silently passing by him is actually an eloquent language of manner that exactly precludes his nearer approach to her by any expression. Her silently passing by may be the only adequate proof that, in fact, she possesses the highest parts of language: wisdom and piety.

Having cited her "higher Beauties," the poem turns to address Mary and to fervently commend her for her dignity and practical common sense in baffling negligible suitors and for controlling her situation (90). The poem reverts to mock-heroic military metaphors to describe how an importunate suitor tries to besiege her by lovers' various ploys. Her situation is, remarkably, a precise counterpart or mirror to the poet's own situation as he had "incamp'd" his mind in the woods, behind trees to ward off Beauty's "Dart" and the world's "Shot" and "Horsemen" (76). And we are induced to infer that Mary and the poet have been circling one another in an extraordinarily subtle and mannerly battle of the sexes. Despite anonymity in the stanza's descriptions, several expressions hint that the suitor or suitors unflatteringly pictured weeping, sighing, and lying possibly include the poet himself (90). That the suitor or suitors are designated "Youth" reminds us that the poet apostrophizes himself by that same name when Mary enters the scene to pass in his vicinity (82). Furthermore, the last and most devious trick the suitor resorts to, an "*Ambush*" of "*feign'd complying Innocence*," not only demands a singular referent but also precisely fits the somewhat ambiguous circumstances of how and why the poet himself comes to be located in this place when Mary walks by (77–78).

Stanza 90 ends by reporting that Mary safely eludes her importunate suitor. And as she escapes by the "roughest Way" the literal situation is that she probably slips into the woods, for we recall that the woods, which also signify her family, serve to conceal her (88). Moreover, quite apart from whatever may be her intimate feelings about the poet's suit, the "roughest Way" also seems to fit her eluding the suitor by resorting to utter silence and flight when her special facility is "to converse / In all the Languages as *hers*" (89). So, she gets away and disappears from the scene and the poet's vicinity, and he loses prospect of their closer relation. He is at last obliged to love her only at a distance. He becomes the evident counterpart to William Fairfax, who might not have broken into the nunnery to carry off Isabel Thwaites as wife. Instead of becoming Mary's "*Love*" the poet becomes her "*Devoto*" (19) and ends his love-ordeal by extolling her perfect purity and goodness.

Perhaps entering its dramatic denoument, the poem goes on to attribute Mary's superior disposition and behavior to her careful nurturing in the family (91). Generally "the safe, but roughest Way" she avoids being overtaken is by her submitting to the family's "*Discipline* severe." It is, no doubt, training authorized in heaven, to which Melville found allusion in the family names: "Of *Fairfax*, and the starry *Vere*." Coming from a family of soldiers, Mary is understandably effective in baffling a suitor's campaign of quasi-military approaches. Altogether, stanza 91 explains that the household secludes her from possible malign influence, especially from predatory males.

Mary is raised in virtual cloister, as if she were an improved

Isabel Thwaites. The explanation that nothing can get to her
there except what is "pure, and spotless as the Eye" significantly
resonates several prior images in the poem. During his deep study
in the woods the poet sees, through the protective, covering brush,
the "hatching *Thrastles* shining Eye," which glares back at him
and prophetically warns him against trying to take Mary (67). In
another instance, the poet leads us to the extreme relativistic
verge of the abyssal meadow where cattle look like spots on faces
and the spots like fleas seen under instruments that, were they
turned, would show us constellations like cattle (58). These paradoxical fluctuations in scale and point of view make usual experience into dizzying illusions from which it is fortunately
possible to flee. The accumulated meaning of these resonant eye-
figures appears to be that mere perceptual experience, including
the foresight or intuition of ruin (67–69), is not in itself damaging. After all, the family ancestor, Isabel Thwaites, was much
more exposed to error than is Mary, with little subsequent stigma
attaching to her. The idea corresponds to Adam's astonishing
moral proposition in Book V of *Paradise Lost*, where he instructs
Eve after her disturbing dream that anticipates her seduction:

> Evil into the mind of God or Man
> May come and go, so unapprov'd, and leave
> No spot or blame behind . . . .

The sense of the whole figure in stanza 91, then, is that raised
within this family and subject to no encroachments beyond mere
speculation, Mary is chaste in her deportment and so her virtue
is spotless. They can't much blame the poet for only looking, or
her either, for that matter. But the stanza's last couplet simultaneously refers both to morality and, by the legalism "intail," to
economics, and it archly reminds us that Mary's reward for correct deportment is that she will inherit great family wealth as she
is the only immediate heir. Thus the entire stanza reaffirms that
the poet owes his own wise and pious bearing in the Fairfax
household to Mary and, beyond her, to her family's coercive
power. His goodness merely mirrors hers and, with some possible
irony, theirs.

As a way to further celebrate Mary's superior values and worth, stanza 92 apostrophizes the opposite type of foolish women who strive only for superficial beauty. That the face alone preoccupies them significantly relates them to the lubricious nuns, who professed to want Isabel as a model for the faces they embroider (16–17). The stanza emphasizes Mary's true studies by attributing "Study" of a sort to women who, ignoring higher knowledge and morality, vainly try only to prevent wrinkles and aging but who are at last rewarded with only mask-like vacant faces that are nearly death's-heads: "Yet your own Face shall at you grin, / Thorough the Black-bag of your Skin." Perhaps these foolish women make faces to win the false, flattering suitors that Mary shuns (90). Contrarily, Mary's study is vital and fulfilling. The stanza's final couplet likens it to cultivation, maybe of the pious sort her father retired to pursue at Appleton House (45). Thus Mary brings more to her family line than only a face and her natural child-bearing prospects (93). "With Graces more divine," she is better endowed than is usual for a woman in her time and station.

Stanza 93 next presents an emblem, not unlike those studied by the poet in the woods, that prophesies her suitable wedding to sustain the family line. The metaphor which compares her to mistletoe, at her marriage to be cut from the parental tree, is somewhat ambivalent in that it figures her separation from family and an ending to part of her life as well as a new beginning. But the entire emblem means fruitful cultivation and is happier in its prospect than its corresponding emblem of the heron dropping its oldest fledgling (67). So, whatever Mary's feelings in the matter, altogether her parents will "most rejoice" to make the sacrifice that will sustain their line. Their being gratified to "make their *Destiny* their *Choice*" again implies that they strictly control Mary's mating. They would be deeply offended should the poet himself take her in mesalliance and thus ruin the family's more noble destiny. In fact we know that in 1657 Mary was wed, to become the Duchess of Buckingham, and that, ironically, her husband was a notorious rake.[5] He was George Villiers, renowned

5. Pierre Legouis, *Andrew Marvell: Poet, Puritan, Patriot*, 2nd ed. (Oxford: Clarendon Press, 1968), p. 19.

for *The Rehearsal,* which satirized heroic tragedies generally and
their authors, including D'Avenant and Dryden, particularly.

Now certainly into its dramatic denouement, the poem returns from its prophecy to its present at Appleton House and
further praises Mary's excellence by proposing her as a model
for the manor's improvement. Stanza 94 apostrophizes the elements of the estate—"Fields, Springs, Bushes, Flow'rs"—to emulate Mary's precedence among women and make themselves
superior to all their kinds. But since this preeminence is already
a major premise, here the poem reaffirms that Mary is the source
and epitome; as in stanza 87, the gardens, woods, meadow, and
river are preferred because they are hers. The effect is a focusing
upon Mary as the center of the world; as she is to Appleton
House, it is to England, and England to the whole world. By
starting with her arrival that abruptly wakes the poet from his
otherworld and back into the conventional social world (82), the
entire last part of the poem implies that Mary turns the world
and that by her it can be improved and redeemed. Like her father
(44), Mary has the power to save the fallen world (41), but she
will not duplicate his destiny. She will instead complement and
complete it. He was nurtured in worldly wars and retired to his
garden for a destiny of private goodness, whereas Mary, his offspring, is nurtured in that cloisteral garden to go out and wed
the world eventually and extend her goodness to it. The poem's
truth is not polarizations; it is not that public values are preferred
to private, nor action to reflection, nor house to woods, nor art to
nature. The truth of this poem, as of its epic precedents, is the
reciprocity and mutuality between these poles. The world's
wholeness is the truth. Earlier in the family line Fairfax strived
for Thwaites; now in the family a Thwaites awaits a Fairfax.

Stanza 95 further apostrophizes the estate and boldly pro-
nounces that it supersedes all sites renowned for beauty, including extreme places representing wanton love and heroic death.
The exotic Spanish place-names which recall the poet's earlier
machines for rapidly changing scenes (56), seem to authenticate
the proposition spatially, and the antique mythical names certify
it through time and beyond. Mostly, however, the strange jumble
of remote geographic and fabulous names and their distressing

confusions of both esthetic and moral values warrants the following stanza's complaint that the world has fallen to disorder (96). The summary that it is "a rude heap together hurl'd" claims the world's nature is as degenerate as its art, its absurd architecture and false epic, reproached at the poem's beginning. But stanza 96 goes on to apostrophize Appleton House as an enclave of order within the wider world's disorder. It is still a little paradise at the world's center, just as all of England once was (41). And of course we continue to appreciate that all this centers in Mary's excellence. The entire stanza, then, succinctly summarizes the poem's regard for Appleton House by acclaiming it the fallen world's exact counterpart: "*You Heaven's Center, Nature's Lap. And Paradice's only Map.*"

The poem ends with a memorable picture of the day's end and nightfall. Fishermen are described coming in off the river, and they are "moist," not unlike the fishes they angle for (97). The reference reminds us that the poet was himself an angler, deeply immersed in his natural circumstance and marvelously commingled with that otherworld, until Mary passed through the scene and recalled him to more sober and conventional imaginative order. The stanza's complex second couplet describes the fishermen, carrying their coracles inverted over their heads and shoulders, as alien beings from an underworld. Such large shoes, moreover, vaguely imply grotesque or titanic creatures. Perhaps the coming darkness obscures and blurs vision so that the identities of objects become ambiguous. The third couplet likens the fishermen carrying boats over their heads to tortoises, which bear their shells on their backs. Additionally named "rational *Amphibii,*" they make a shadowy tableau of beasts come up from the river to prowl the earth at night. Such a picture seems apposite to the preceding stanza's representation of the wrecked world surrounding Appleton House. Like the poem's watery flood earlier (60), a new flood of darkness now disorders the world. And in the last couplet the dark heavens overhead are threatening because they seem like the monstrous amphibian swollen to titanic size. Or if the couplet conversely represents only the dark hemispheric shell, we recall the poem's first tortoises and fearfully wonder what creature's body measures out this place (2).

The poem begins by criticizing unproportioned, extravagant dwellings that do not suit their occupants, on the grounds that such art belies nature and is false. And now the poem ends with a fearful recognition that part of the truth about the world and nature is that it can be alien and threateningly not human, although the horrors may be subjective as much as objective. In fact, just such recognitions explain why human beings so prize sheltering sanctuaries, build dwellings for themselves, and create works of art such as gardens and poems.[6] At last the poem's gradual end of day and onset of night suddenly prompt the poet's imagination to a frightened turning. This final dark vision impels him to leave the woods and stream, the most natural and ambiguous locations in the estate, and to lead us back in to the house itself.

Having become accustomed to the sheltered life at Appleton House, the poet, during the day of this poem, leads us far out into the estate. There he elliptically discloses that he has gone as far as to fall in love with Mary and to think of abducting her, an action that would ruin the house. All this adventure out from the center, both his falling in love and the day's disclosures and discoveries, is, however, inside experience in several ways. It occurs at all because the poet has been taken into the household and enjoys its prerogatives, especially its idyllic sanctuary. It is also inside experience in that it is principally contained within the poet's imagination. The freedom of the adventure—its elisions and fluidity, its play with scale and perspective—locate the day's experiences in his mind as much as the English landscape. But this latter imaginative adventuring is at last so fluid and daring that it brings him to startled awareness of an entire outside counterpart, alien to his inside life. Suddenly menaced, he appreciates the comforting worth of his inside situation and is confirmed in his earlier sentiment not to take Mary. Paradoxically, his outward adventure saves him from irrecoverable extravagance. His ultimate act of allegiance and compliment to Appleton House is his impulsive turning at last to go back in.

6. Northrop Frye's address to these human impulses is especially pertinent. "Motive for Metaphor," *The Educated Imagination* (Bloomington: Indiana University Press, 1964), pp. 11–33.

modern

Picasso, "Boy Holding a Blue Vase," ca. 1900.
Courtesy of the Hyde Collection, Glens Falls, New York

6

The Observer Observed:
Notes on the Narrator of *Under Western Eyes*

Donald R. Swanson

Joseph Conrad's novel concerning Russia and Russians would have been a very different affair had he held to his original plan. But in the actual working out of his story, he significantly shifted its focus of narration, and thus also the meaning and effect of the whole.

On January 6, 1908, Conrad wrote a letter to his friend Galsworthy in which he described the first steps in the writing of his new novel. The title, he said, was to be *Razumov*. "Isn't it expressive? I think that I am trying to capture the very soul of things Russian,—*Cosas de Russia*. It is not an easy work but it may be rather good when it's done." The letter also contained a brief synopsis of the plot which Conrad called the "theme." It focussed upon a "Student Razumov," the natural son of "a Prince K," who secretly hands over to the police a fellow student, Haldin, a political murderer. Haldin is subsequently captured and hanged.

Going abroad to Geneva, Razumov (apparently by chance) meets Haldin's mother and sister. He falls in love with the sister, they are married, and some years later he confesses to her his part in her brother's death. "The psychological developments leading to Razumov's betrayal of Haldin, to the confession of the fact to his wife and to the death of these people (brought about

109

mainly by the resemblance of their child to the late Haldin), form the real subject of the story."[1]

In the writing of the novel, Conrad stuck close to his original plan only in "Part First," which constitutes about one quarter of the novel. Here the action centers upon the experiences of Razumov in St. Petersburg. But even this part is substantially altered in meaning and in focus by its opening section, in which a narrator is introduced—an English teacher of languages, resident in Geneva. How he happens to be telling the story emerges gradually during the entire course of the novel. In spite of Conrad's insistence to the contrary, the story is concerned not so much with the nature of things Russian as it is with the way a Westerner—as the title of the finished work suggests—thinks of them. By the time the novel was completed, *Razumov* was no longer an appropriate title. The principal focus of *Under Western Eyes* is upon the foreign witness to the events.

Conrad has used narrators in some of his other stories for a variety of purposes. A narrator interposed between the story and the reader can help to give both distance and verisimilitude, and can act as a connecting link between cultures or generations. In "The Lagoon," the "white man" is the listener to Arsat's story and acts as a link between the Malay culture that Arsat describes and Conrad's English audience. The "white man's" presence in the story prevents the reader from too easily universalizing and identifying with the characters and events: one is never permitted to forget that the characters and their society are "Eastern"—that is, different.

In stories such as "Prince Roman" and "Il Conde," the narrator is both the reader's proxy within the story and the interpreter of events surrounding the tale that he has heard from someone else. *Lord Jim* is related by "Marlow" at a distance from the action in which he himself is little involved. The narrative situation in *Heart of Darkness* and in the short story "Youth," however, is rather different.

Heart of Darkness is told indirectly by an unnamed first-

1. G. Jean-Aubry, *Joseph Conrad: Life and Letters* (New York: Doubleday, 1927), II, 64–65.

person narrator who, in turn, tells of his being on the deck of the cruising yawl *Nellie* with several others, among whom is Marlow, who tells the story. This kind of narrative layering is not at all new; it is the device used, for example, in the *Canterbury Tales*. It allows for complexity—and some confusion—in point of view, since the reader cannot with certainty tell at what layer of narration judgments are made. In "Youth," again, Conrad makes use of the unnamed first-person narrator who reports at second hand a story told by Marlow. In both of these instances, Marlow is recounting his own past experiences, in "Youth" the experiences he had in the distant past.

It is the nature of the narrator that gives "Youth" its theme. Marlow at the age of forty-two is trying to explain to his old friends, and apparently to himself as well, the nature of Marlow at twenty, from which he abstracts certain characteristics of "youth." At twenty, Marlow was active, romantic, thoughtless— or at least that is what is remembered by the older, contemplative Marlow. But does he remember accurately? It is in the nature of recollection to be selective, and the Marlow who says "Ah, youth!" seems to have forgotten all the pain, suffering, and doubt that accompanied the actions he describes. One of the ironies of the story is that the narrator is at least as much a romanticizer as the young Marlow. The younger man is a fictional creation of his older self. His life is given order and meaning by the selection and arrangement of memories on the part of the older Marlow; it is given significant form which enables the narrator to deduce the theme around which the action of the story revolves.

In *Under Western Eyes* the narrator, an "elderly Englishman," provides a number of contrasts to Razumov. First, his age contrasts with Razumov's youth. Then his "Western" mind, like the mind of the "white man" in "The Lagoon," imperfectly comprehends the events of a familiar but alien culture which he must try to understand and, in the case of the narrator of *Under Western Eyes*, must try to explain to his audience. And, in the confusion of documents and other sources from which his information is taken, the origin of the evaluations of events reported by the narrator of *Under Western Eyes* is lost to the reader. One knows only that the bulk of the information that does not derive from the narrator's first-hand experience comes from Razumov's "secret diaries."

In elucidating the "psychological developments" in his Russian characters for his English audience, Conrad has resorted to an English narrator who acts, in part, like Carlyle's "Editor" in *Sartor Resartus,* who reports the events in the life of "Professor Diogenes Teufelsdröckh" mainly through "documents" provided him by a friend of the Professor.[2] In support of his own veracity, Conrad's narrator explains that "this is not a work of imagination; I have no talent; my excuse for this undertaking lies not in its art, but in its artlessness."[3] Indeed, he protests too much, and one soon suspects the crafty old teacher of being more artful than he would like to appear. The elaborate interweaving of the materials that make up *Under Western Eyes* reflects not only upon the skill of Conrad as a storyteller, but also upon the narrative sense of his created persona, the English teacher of languages.

The narrator of *Under Western Eyes* discloses a number of his own personality traits during the course of the story which directly effect the way in which he tells it. He is first of all a teacher of languages who, until the age of nine, had himself lived in St. Petersburg, but whose knowledge of the Russian language derives mostly from his later studies. He is a bachelor who at the time of Razumov's arrival in Geneva had lived for ten years in three rented rooms, part of the apartment of the widow of a distinguished professor in that city. He is also susceptible to the charms of young women, as he shows frequently in his references to Nathalie Haldin, yet he is a solitary person who habitually "dines alone." He is fluent in the Russian language, but finds the "Russian soul" incomprehensible. He is English, yet his only contact with English people is when he walks a short distance with Razumov on his way to the railway station to meet a visitor from England. A short time later he sees Razumov again near the post

2. Conrad read *Sartor Resartus* at least once, probably more than once. See reference in "Youth."
3. Joseph Conrad, *Under Western Eyes* (Garden City, N.Y.: Doubleday, 1963), p. 84. Subsequent references are to this edition, and page numbers of excerpts are given parenthetically in the text.

office. He is returning from the railway station, but no English companion is in evidence. In fact, the narrator is pointedly alone.

Razumov is mysterious to most of the other characters in the novel, but it is the narrator who is more mysterious to the reader. This is probably a principal reason why many readers resent the existence of the narrator at all. They want to get on with the adventures of Razumov, and they dislike the intrusion of this perplexing and apparently extraneous personage.

Yet he is not really extraneous. Conrad makes him the key to the whole novel—not *just* a narrative device, but a receiver, transmitter, and interpreter to the Western reader of the Russian soul, Russian thought, and the Russian political system. He is manifestly fallible in his judgments, and often admits to the reader his perplexities. He thinks that he agrees with Razumov in some important respects. He is "liberal," but not *too* liberal. He views autocracy as one form of lawlessness and revolution as another. Yet he is not entirely happy with Genevan democracy either. If Russia is horrible, Switzerland is dull. And yet, he can live safely in Switzerland.

In his focus upon Razumov, Conrad is trying to explain "the very soul of things Russian"; in his focus upon the narrator, he provides an interpreter who may perhaps make at least some of this explanation intelligible to the Western reader. In the process, Razumov's story (including some of its psychological aspects) becomes clear enough, but another dimension of mystery is added. Who and what *is* this curious Englishman?

He is, of course, first of all a rhetorical device. Conrad frequently interposes his narrators between story and reader, and whenever there is a danger that the reader will become too absorbed in the action, the narrator recalls him to the fact that a story is being told. "Pass the bottle!" Marlow says periodically during the course of "Youth," which recalls the reader from the adventure to the middle-aged gentlemen sitting around a table listening to Marlow speak. Attention shifts from the story to the storyteller, a man with certain characteristics who has led a certain kind of life. He is telling in his own special way an old story of universal significance: youth is a time for action; maturity is a time for contemplation. But the older Marlow is what he is *be-*

cause of the particular experiences he had when he was younger; he contemplates life according to his experience.

Quite a different situation exists in *Under Western Eyes.* The storyteller and the person about whom the story is told are not only of different ages; they are of different worlds. Whatever kind of life the narrator had led in his youth, it could not in the nature of things have resembled Razumov's life. He is English— Western. Liberal democracy (epitomized by Switzerland) has informed his whole experience. He knows Russian autocracy only intellectually and at second hand. Despite his early residence in Russia, as an English—and therefore privileged—child, he has no *experience* of the meaning of this autocracy.

Razumov, on the other hand, owes everything to the Russian autocratic state. Born the illegitimate son of a nobleman who has served the tsar according to his class and understanding, Razumov passes his youth in solitary relationship to the Russian nation and state. He has no acknowledged family. Therefore, as he thinks almost incessantly, he is a Russian or nothing: "Russia *can't* disown me. She cannot! . . . I am *it!*" (p. 176). He studies Russian law; he is caught up in a Russian political situation in spite of himself; he becomes an agent of the imperial secret police while ostensibly a revolutionary and a terrorist. He hates and fears both the revolutionists and the police he serves; he would like only to continue his studies. An English life would have suited him, but his Russian experience has made that psychologically impossible.

The narrator tries but cannot really understand all this. He is a rather pedantic scholar who has assembled certain data which he presents to the reader, together with his comments upon the nature of this work, the limits of his abilities, and occasional digressions concerning life, politics, society, and other matters, after the fashion of Swift's *Tale of a Tub* and Carlyle's *Sartor Resartus.* At the beginning of the novel, Conrad establishes the persona through whom his story is to be presented:

> To begin with I wish to disclaim the possession of those high gifts of imagination and expression which would have enabled my pen to create for the reader the personality of the man who called

himself, after the Russian custom, Cyril, son of Isador—Kirylo Sidorovitch—Razumov.

If I have ever had these gifts in any sort of living form they have been smothered out of existence a long time ago under a wilderness of words. Words, as is well known, are the great foes of reality. (p. 1)

The speaker goes on to explain that he is a teacher of languages, "an occupation which at length becomes fatal to whatever share of imagination, observation, and insight an ordinary person may be heir to."

The narrator puts forward his particular failings as reasons why the reader should believe in the accuracy and truth of the following pages: "I could not have observed Mr. Razumov or guessed at his reality by the force of insight, much less have imagined him as he was. Even to invent the mere bald facts of his life would have been utterly beyond my powers. But I think that without this declaration the readers of these pages will be able to detect in the story the marks of documentary evidence. . . . It is based on a document" (p. 1).

The document is "something in the nature of a journal, a diary, yet not exactly that in its actual form." Though the entries are dated, most of it was not written from day to day but in large sections, sometimes covering several months. "All the earlier part is retrospect, in a narrative form, relating to an event which took place about a year before."

From this, the narrator explains something of his own background, mostly in relation to his knowledge of Russians. "I confess," he says, "that I have no comprehension of the Russian character," which he then discusses in a short digression. From this, Conrad's narrator drifts into speculation about why Razumov wrote such a dangerously self-incriminating document, but he does not tell how he came by it until nearly the end of the novel. First, he sketches what he knows about Razumov's background, and then he turns to the experiences of the student Razumov in St. Petersburg.

The narrator disclaims both the ability and the intention to create a work of art or imagination. Yet he takes Razumov's story told in "retrospect, in a narrative form," and not only translates it into English, but retells it from the outside, in the third person. Some of this is summary narrative, some is presented in direct scenes with dialogue. One is left to wonder whether Razumov is supposed to have recorded these conversations in detail, long after the fact, or whether the narrator is not being more imaginative than he pretends to be. For Conrad has created the character of the narrator and his situation, and it is not idle to wonder at the veracity of the narrator when he tells of the method by which he composed this complex work.

Frequently, as in the case of Marlow's narration in "Youth," the interest of the story itself is enough to obliterate the narrator from the mind of the reader. And also, as in "Youth," Conrad periodically reminds the reader of the narrator's presence. After Haldin has left Razumov's room to walk into the police trap, his betrayer falls into "a leaden sleep." What will happen next? At this crisis the narrator breaks into the story again: "Approaching this part of Mr. Razumov's story, my mind, the decent mind of an old teacher of languages, feels more and more the difficulty of the task" (p. 55). Conrad breaks his story because of the danger that the reader may be following the story for Razumov's adventure itself, but it is not the adventure that Conrad wants him to be concerned about. As the novelist wrote to Galsworthy, "I want to capture the very soul of things Russian"; he does not want merely to characterize a particular man in unique circumstances. As the narrator points out: "The task is not in truth the writing in the narrative form a précis of a strange human document, but the rendering—I perceive it now clearly—of the moral conditions ruling over a large portion of this earth's surface; conditions not easily to be understood, much less discovered in the limits of a story, till some key-word is found; a word that could stand at the back of all the words covering the pages, a word which, if not truth itself, may perchance hold truth enough to help the moral discovery which should be the object of every tale" (p. 55).

The word that the narrator, and probably Conrad as well, finds as a "key-word" that can "help the moral discovery" in this tale is *cynicism*. It characterizes the actions not only of the supporters of Russian autocracy, but the actions of most of the revolutionists as well. It is the quality that is lacking in the idealistic Haldin as well as in his sister. And finally, it is lack of sufficient cynicism that leads to the destruction, or rather transformation, of Razumov. Because neither Razumov nor Nathalie Haldin is destroyed in the novel, they are simply morally (and in the case of Razumov, physically as well) shattered, and subsequently, upon their separate returns to Russia, absorbed into the "cynical" system.

But the reader can see this largely because the narrator remains at a distance from the emotions that govern the lives of the principal characters. If he himself remains rather obscure, he helps to clarify the actions of others even while disclaiming any understanding of "the Russian character."

Structurally, the novel is divided into four parts. The first part, ostensibly based upon Razumov's summary account of his past experiences, deals with his experience in St. Petersburg. Parts two and three deal with the events, about a year later, in Geneva, while the fourth part returns to Razumov's encounter with Councillor Mikulin before he left Russia, and goes forward to the events that follow the Geneva adventures. It is here that the reader finally learns that the diaries were sent by Razumov to Nathalie Haldin on the night of his confessions, and were given by her to the narrator when she was about to return to Russia. The documentary evidence is nearly complete. All that is needed is the disclosure of the source of the narrator's information concerning the later experiences of Nathalie and of the crippled Razumov, which the reader learns was given to the narrator by the revolutionist Sophia Antonovna whom he meets when she returns to Geneva during her travels.

At the beginning of "Part Second," the narrator still feels compelled to disclaim any "imagination"; he does not want to be accused of creativity. "In the conduct of an invented story there are, no doubt, certain proprieties to be observed for the sake of clearness and effect. A man of imagination, however inexperienced in the art of narrative, has his instinct to guide him in the choice of his words, and in the development of the action. . . . But this is not a work of imagination; I have no talent; my excuse for this undertaking lies not in its art, but in its artlessness" (p. 84). The narrator claims no more than "the sincerity of my purpose."

Part of the meaning of this novel is the tension between the story being told and the teller of it; between the attempt to maintain verisimilitude (on several levels) and the obvious fact that the reader is reading "fiction." But fiction through which a theme is presented is an important form of truth; more obviously true, paradoxically, when the reader is kept aware of the fiction through which the general truth of the theme is presented. One of the ways in which Conrad keeps his reader aware of the fictional nature of some of his stories, as well as of the essential truth behind the fictions, is by the creation of often elaborately contrived narrators such as the elderly English gentleman in *Under Western Eyes.*

7

Ulysses as Ghost Story

SANFORD PINSKER
—Tell us a story, sir.
—Oh, do, sir, a ghoststory.
from *Ulysses*

IN THE "NESTOR" SECTION of *Ulysses*, Stephen Dedalus' students, like our own, prefer entertainment to rigorous work, a "ghoststory" rather than a history lesson. Stephen gives them both, albeit from an oblique angle. In a chapter which begins, significantly, with a discussion of Pyrrhus and ends with the Pyrrhic victory of Mr. Deasy's "dancing coins," Stephen equates uneasy spirits from the past with the quotidian reality of Dublin on 16 June 1904. And as "history" gives way to "literature," the elegiac tone of Milton's "Lycidas" collapses the distance between the restless, inattentive students and the deeper restlessness of their teacher. For Stephen, every historical example, every literary allusion contributes one more bitter lesson to his growing disenchantment with the present moment.

The pressures outlined above are capsulized in Stephen's sweeping pronouncement that "History is a nightmare from which I am trying to awake."[1] Time, in effect, plays the cheat, restricting

1. James Joyce, *Ulysses* (New York: Random House, 1961), p. 34. Subsequent references are to this edition, and page numbers of excerpts are given parenthetically in the text.

infinite possibilities to those things which actually were. Rage as he will, that which was, *was;* that which is, *is:* "Had Pyrrhus not fallen by a beldam's hand in Argos or Julius Ceasar not been knifed to death? They are not to be thought away. Time has branded them and fettered they are lodged in the room of the infinite possibilities they have ousted. But can those have been possible seeing that they never were? Or was that only possible which came to pass?" (p. 25). Earlier, the boorishly insensitive Haines attempts to deflate Stephen's floating disenchantment with history. As he condescendingly puts it: "We feel in England that we have treated you rather unfairly. It seems history is to blame" (p. 20).

For Haines, "history" is an impersonal, which is to say *academic*, affair, safely disconnected from his cultural raids on Irish folklore or highly symbolic "smooth silver [cigarette] case in which twinkled a green stone" (pp. 19–20). Stephen, on the other hand, feels the oppressive weight of "two masters"—the "imperial British state and the holy Roman catholic and apostolic church" (p. 20). In another country, Saul Bellow's Herzog could quip that oppressed people tend to be witty; in Stephen's case, however, oppression makes him testy as well, torn between lashing out at a smug Haines or lashing inward at an ineffectual self. As an avatar of Telemachus, his internalized "Usurper!" is an anguished acknowledgment of the assorted ghosts which haunt the novel's opening chapter.

But such broadly defined socio-political "ghosts" are not the whole story, even for an ambivalent national like Stephen. In *A Portrait of the Artist as a Young Man*, the nets which would place a low ceiling over an aspiring artist are three fold. As Stephen— inordinately attracted to trinities, by training and inclination— puts it: "When the soul of a man is born in this country there are nets flung at it to hold it back from flight. You talk to me of nationality, language, religion. I shall try to fly by those nets."[2]

The liberations presumably necessary for one to become an artist complete the process of maturation outlined in a *kunstler-*

2. James Joyce, *A Portrait of the Artist as a Young Man* (New York: Viking, 1956), p. 203. Subsequent references are to this edition, and page numbers of excerpts are given parenthetically in the text.

roman. Stephen moves from the pains of childhood, through the stations of religious dogma, to the making of a self-styled esthetic theory. In effect, he turns the old catechisms upside-down, becoming a "priest of eternal imagination," one capable of "transmuting the daily bread of experience into the radiant body of everlasting life" (p. 221). Terms appropriated from Aquinas— *integritas, consonantia* and *claritas*—metamorphose, somewhat uneasily, into erudite talk about the epical, lyrical, and dramatic modes.

The dazzling convolutions of Stephen's esthetics cannot help but impress the likes of Lynch, however much their "scholastic stink" seems airy stuff. With Cranly, however, Stephen adds Trinities with grittier implications. The result has just the right touch of Satanic bravado and desperate risk that we associate with a Romantic protagonist out to "suffer" for his Art: "Look here, Cranly, . . . You have asked me what I would do and what I would not do. . . . I will not serve that in which I no longer believe whether it call itself my home, my fatherland, or my church: and I will try to express myself in some mode of life or art as freely as I can and as wholly as I can, using for my defense the only arms I allow myself to use—silence, exile, and cunning" (pp. 246–47).

Stephen, in effect, tries out his new-found wings by systematically reducing his "friends" to sounding boards for a grand esthetic theory. Stephen turns increasingly solipsistic, always threatening to collapse the fabric of shared discourse into self-congratulatory monolog. Such a program can only end with the special silences of a private journal, that diary in which Stephen records the transition from flights of fancy to one of fact.

But mere resistance does not always equal heroism, nor does a self-styled exile foreshadow stunning success. The *Portrait* is less a study in the growth of Stephen's soul than it is an etiquette book for other would-be artists equally misunderstood by parents, preachers, teachers, firemen, and cops. *Ulysses* tells a very different story, but for readers who thrill to the rhetoric of adolescent posturing, Stephen is the stuff of which pop-hero posters are made.

Joyce, however, stressed the last four words of his title (*as*

a Young Man), suggesting something of the irony he interposed
between a pretentious esthete and a comprehensive vision. For
example, it is difficult to think of literary works which would *not*
fit into Stephen's labored categories of the epical, lyrical, and
dramatic. It is even more difficult to think of literary works which
are not bound to the concerns of family, church, and state. In
short, by divorcing himself from the only subjects *worth* writing
about—or, indeed, that one *can* write about—Stephen divorces
himself from the very sources of art. Stephen's complicated the-
ories are headier, even more interesting, than most, but it is a
good deal easier to talk about art than to do it, easier to fashion
large promises than fulfill them.

Unfortunately, what the Stephen of *Ulysses* calls "agenbite
of inwit" (remorse of conscience) is less a matter of creative un-
fulfillment than it is a study in the anguish wrestling with the
residues of intellectual principle. That he "will not serve" may
establish Stephen's uncompromising integrity, but such fateful
decisions are never made in the pristine, coldly academic innocence that Stephen imagines. And this is doubly true if the issue
pits the truths of Stephen's head against the deeper ones of his
mother's heart. In that closed system called the *Portrait,* the
choice seems resoundingly clear:

> She [Stephen's mother] wished me to make my Easter duty.
> —And will you?
> —I will not. . . . I will not serve, answered Stephen.
>
> (p. 239)

Cranly tries to suggest something of the heart's need in his
final conversation with Stephen, but without success. Self-righ-
teousness and a flair for scholastic argument will always sidetrack
appeals to the bottom line. And, too, Stephen has grown testy
enough to enjoy the capital A, Alienation:

> —Whatever else is unsure in this stinking dunghill of a world
> a mother's love is not. Your mother brings you into the world,
> carries you first in her body. What do we know about what she
> feels? But whatever she feels, it, at least, must be real. . . .

—Pascal, if I remember rightly, would not suffer his mother to kiss him as he feared the contact of her sex.

—Pascal was a pig, said Cranly.

—Aloysius Gonzaga, I think, was of the same mind, Stephen said.

—And he was another pig then, said Cranly.

—The church calls him a saint.

(pp. 241–42)

Ulysses tests out the hidden costs of Stephen's esthetic program. It is also a book in which a comic "father" discovers that he can teach and a reluctant "son" discovers that he can learn. Like all genuine instruction, the lessons are a matter of unspectacular moments gradually accumulated, rather than sudden, blinding flashes. Stephen begins his sojourn in *Ulysses* by raking at the ashes of consequence, haunted by the ghost of a mother he had refused on principle. Half a procrastinating Hamlet, half an ineffectual Telemachus, Stephen finds himself caught in the crunch between an artistic future even he has begun to doubt and a personal past he is afraid to face.

In *Ulysses*, Stephen's present is reduced to nearly equal doses of frustration and contempt. His ongoing autobiography is, in effect, a "ghoststory," one which plays regret against the backdrop of spectral horrors: "In a dream, silently, she [his mother] had come to him, her wasted body within its loose graveclothes giving off an odour of wax and rosewood, her breath bent over him with mute secret words, a faint odour of wetted ashes" (p. 10). Moreover, his perplexing "riddle" about a poor soul going to heaven as the "bells . . . / Were striking eleven" is given an even more perplexing *answer:* "The fox burying his grandmother under a hollybush" (p. 27). It is hardly surprising that Stephen's students find themselves befuddled. Art is, among other things, a disguise, a way of simultaneously concealing and revealing. In the Library section, Stephen distinguishes between "that player Shakespeare, a ghost by absence" and King Hamlet, a "ghost by death" (p. 189). But his ingenious attempt to unlock *Hamlet's* mystery via algebra—like the sardonic fox and grandmother offered earlier—is addressed to ghosts more personally immediate than literary. Stephen's elaborate theory about *Hamlet* is an exercise aimed at replacing the hard facts of his own paternity (the father, a ghost by absence; the mother, a ghost by death) with more attractive myths about self-creation.

Ironically, such verbal pyrotechnics only increases the anguish of Stephen's position. It is easier to dismiss one's father by invoking the formula that "paternity may be a legal fiction" (p. 207) than it is to expunge that more quotidian navel Stephen mused about in "Proteus":

> The cords of all link back, standentwining cable of all flesh. That is why mystic monks. Will you be as gods? Gaze in your omphalos. . . .
> Spouse and helpmate of Adam Kadman: Heva, naked Eve. She had no navel. Gaze. Belly without blemish, bulging big, a buckler of taut vellum, no, whiteheaped corn, orient and immortal, standing from everlasting to everlasting. Womb of sin.
> Wombed in sin darkness I was too, made not begotten. By them, the man with my voice and eyes and a ghostwoman with ashes on her breath. (p. 38)

In "Proteus," that convoluted stream-of-consciousness we associate with Stephen swirls through a largely disembodied brain. That is, Stephen confronts the shards of his past with all the vengeance scholasticism can muster. Rather than the confident bravado which ended the *Portrait*—"Welcome, O Life! I go to encounter for the millionth time the reality of experience"— Stephen turns, á la Proteus, into an Icarus redux nearing the end of complexity's tether. He may have encountered something of the "reality of experience," but to assimilate its meaning requires that necessary antithesis known as Bloom.

Put another way: Stephen juxtaposes a reading list which runs the gamut from "the fading prophecies of Joachim Abbas" (p. 39) to *La vie de Jésus* by M. Leo Taxil with a running account of his Parisian failures. After wrestling with Stephen's airy shape-shifting—"Disguises, clutched at, gone, not here" (p. 43)— we are relieved to discover that "Kidneys were in his [Bloom's] mind" (p. 55). If Stephen's emblematic word is an icy "No!" Bloom's is an enthusiastic "Maybe." The heart—rather than the mind—dominates his bumbling attempts to understand a universe flooded with raw data. As one of his fellow Dubliners points out, there is, indeed, a touch of the poet about old Bloom. He is a man alternately blessed and cursed by vision. No event, however casual, flows past him unnoticed or unspeculated about. Being Bloom, he cannot act otherwise. For Stephen, all the world seems an extension of the library, an occasion for heady rumination; for Bloom, phenomena are the stuff of which a potential ad, a money-making scheme, or a running commentary on the human condition is made. In "Lotus Eaters," for example, Bloom watches others take communion with an eye as objectively skeptical as it is curiously impressed:

> He stood aside watching their blind masks pass down the aisle, one by one, and seek their places. He approached a bench and seated himself in its corner, nursing his hat and newspaper. These pots we have to wear. We ought to have hats modelled on our heads. They were about him here and there, with heads still bowed in their crimson halters, waiting for it [i.e., the communion wafer] to melt in their stomachs. Something like those mazzoth: it's that sort of bread: unleavened shewbread. Look at them. Now I bet it makes them feel happy. Lollipop. It does. Yes, bread of angels it's called. There's a big idea behind it.   (pp. 80–81)

As Joyce's own title, T. S. Eliot, and two generations of Joyce criticism have demonstrated, the "big idea" is myth. "Metempsychosis"—what Molly delightfully fractures into "met him pike hoses" and Bloom solemnly translates as "the transmigration of souls" (p. 64)—provides the mechanism by which Bloom, Stephen, and Molly are turned into avatars of Odysseus, Telemachus, and Penelope.

But that much said by way of paying tribute to the persistence of Joycean de-coders, it is the "ghoststory" of Bloom-Stephen-Molly which finally matters. The mythic substructure interpenetrates the Dublin of 16 June 1904, reminding us, ghost-like, of larger men, nobler actions. And, yet, Bloom strikes us as more lovable than ridiculous, as inflated by the comparisons to Odysseus as he is diminished by them. For those critics who grow weary of the priggish Stephen and wonder if Molly is the sort of "Earth Mother" one would like to meet after a hard day at the lectern, Bloom becomes doubly attractive. As the Veiled Sibyl of "Circe" puts it: "I'm a Bloomite and I glory in it. I believe in him in spite of all. I'd give my life for him, the funniest man on earth" (p. 491).

If Stephen is haunted by the consciously archaic formula he calls "agenbite of inwit," Bloom spends the bulk of *his* day warding off thoughts of an impending cuckoldry. Whatever else Blazes Boylan might be (Romanticism's "natural man," the Freudian *Sceptre* rather than the accidental "Throwaway," etc.) he is more flesh than apparition, one who will disrupt Bloom's household at precisely 4 P.M. The bold handwriting of his letter to Mrs. Marion Bloom is all too clear.

In a world where even Bloom's "Plasto's high grade ha [t band]" (p. 56) seems to be laughing at him, the cuckolded husband is a public event, the butt of cruel jokes from people like McCoy:

> —My wife has just got an engagement. [McCoy announces, attempting to work his infamous "valise tack" on the wary Bloom] At least it's not settled yet. . . .
> —My wife too, he said. She's going to sing at a swagger affair in the Ulster hall, Belfast on the twentyfifth.
> —That so? McCoy said. Glad to hear that, old man. Who's getting it up? (p. 75)

As McCoy's pointed remark—more *double entendre* than authentic question—ripples through Dublin's impolite society, Bloom throws his normally active mind into an even higher gear. During the carriage ride to Dignam's funeral, for example, Bloom's discomfort is a study in good intentions crowded, uneasily, into small-minded spaces. Simon Dedalus directs vaguely anti-Semitic remarks toward Bloom while Mr. Power hectors his companions about a suicide being "the greatest disgrace to have in the family" (p. 96). However ambivalent Bloom may be about "Jewishness," he cannot avoid the painful fact of his own father's suicide. The tensions that result crackle just under the surface,

at a place where external pressure gives way to the recognition
of internal monologue:

> —But the worst of all, Mr. Power said, is the man who takes his
> own life. . . .
> —Temporary insanity, of course, Martin Cunningham said
> decisively. We must take a charitable view of it.
> —They say a man who does it is a coward, Mr. Dedalus said.
> —It is not for us to judge, Martin Cunningham said.
> Mr. Bloom, about to speak, closed his lips again. . . . They have
> no mercy on that [i.e., suicide] here or infanticide. Refuse chris-
> tian burial. They used to drive a stake of wood through his heart
> in the grave. As if it wasn't broken already.   (p. 96)

In an exhausting day which juxtaposes the minutiae of an
ad unobtained (a key disappointment!) or a library book still
unreturned against the deeper rhythms of a funeral and a birth,
it is with the ghosts of the heart that Stephen, Bloom, and Molly
must fashion a tentative peace. Perhaps the clearest index of difference between Stephen and Bloom lies in their attitudes toward
the respective "ghosts" which haunt them from the grave.
Stephen is stuck in an archetypal sonhood, one which makes forward motion impossible. Bloom, on the other hand, is simultaneously the heir of the suicide Rudolph Virag and father of the
deceased Rudy Bloom. In "Hades," he learns something about the
painful but necessary business of confronting death clearly, without recourse to either rehearsed responses or mawkish clichés.

Moreover, that condition Buck Mulligan flippantly identified
as g.p.i. ("general paralysis of the insane," p. 6) is spread wider
than even he had imagined. Its victims include not only eccentrics
like Casel Boyle O'Connor Fitzmaurice Tisdall Farrell or cranks
like Dennis Breen, but the more introspective as well. Martin
Cunningham's humane equation of suicide with "temporary in-
sanity" is not lost upon the guilt-ridden, anxious Bloom. Mental
breakdown is, indeed, a live possibility in the modern world, one
Bloom tries to ward off by an increasingly energized "busy work"
of the mind. Granted, his meditations are filled with misinforma-
tion and pseudo-science, with a "history" that always threatens

to dissolve into self-constructed myth. In the newspaper office, for example, Bloom watches a typesetter work on a story about Dignam's funeral and zig-zags his way through the following associations:

> mangiD. kcirtaP. Poor papa with his hagadah book, reading backwards with his finger to me. Pessach. Next year in Jerusalem. Dear, O dear! All that long business about that brought us out of the land of Egypt and into the house of bondage *alleluia. Shema Israel Adonai Elohenu.* No, that's the other. Then the twelve brothers, Jacob's sons. And then the lamb and the cat and the dog and the stick and the water and the butcher and the angel of death kills the butcher and he kills the ox and the god kills the cat. Sounds a bit silly till you come to look into it well. Justice it means but it's everybody eating everyone else. That's what life is after all.   (p. 122)

After a day filled with crossed purposes and half-meetings, Stephen and Bloom confront their respective ghosts in Nighttown. More importantly, the needs which have drawn a surrogate father toward a surrogate son are "resolved" at last—albeit, in symbolic counters rather than actual fact. Stephen has it out with his mother, as the "Dance of Death" whirls him into that full-blown hallucination he has been avoiding:

> (*Stephen's mother, emaciated, rises stark through the floor in leper grey with a wreath of faded orange blossoms and a torn bridal veil, her face worn and noseless, green with grave mould. Her hair is scant and lank. She fixes her bluecircled hollow eyesockets on Stephen and opens her toothless mouth uttering a silent word. A choir of virgins and confessors sing voicelessly.*) . . .

THE MOTHER

> (*With the subtle smile of death's madness.*) I was once the beautiful May Goulding. I am dead.   (pp. 579–80)

Bloom, on the other hand, is systematically stripped of psychological defenses, forced to realize that Boylan is as much his own creation as he is his "victimizer." Bloom needs to be a cuckold every bit as much as Molly, presumably, requires a lover. The dance-like motions of guilt and punishment are a mirror image of Stephen's obsession with mortality. The difference rests in Bloom's ability to climb out of personal despair, to replace solipsism with compassion, egotism with love.

Joyce cannot resist the impulse to be ironic at such moments. In "Circe" large insights and maudlin configurations achieve a curious equipoise. As Stephen—once again martyred on behalf of Art—babbles lines from Yeats' "Who Will Drive With Fergus" (the song he sang for his mother, as opposed to the prayers he would not), Bloom, characteristically, misinterprets: "Face reminds me of his poor mother. In the shady wood. The deep white breast. Ferguson, I think I caught. A girl. Some girl. Best thing could happen to him" (p. 609).

Even more importantly, for a chapter in which the psyche can instantly materialize its deepest projections, the final tableau insists too much about the relationship between Pythagorean notions of eleven as an integer of renewal and its effect upon Rudy-cum-Stephen:

> . . . *Against the dark wall a figure appears slowly, a fairy boy of eleven, a changeling, kidnapped, dressed in an Eton suit with glass shoes and a little bronze helmet, holding a book in his hand. He reads from right to left inaudibly, smiling, kissing the page.)*

BLOOM

(*Wonderstruck, calls inaudibly.*) Rudy! (p. 609)

However unsuccessfully, Blephen and Stoom (Joyce's playful way of interchanging jewgreek and greekjew) joust with the world of getting and spending. Molly, on the other hand, seems circumscribed by her bed. Casual readers often equate Bloom's fantasized list of her "lovers" (a series which runs the gamut of Dublin society, including such unlikely candidates as a "bootblack at the General Post Office," p. 731) with the ribald truth about Molly. After all, here is an earthy character, full of the swagger we associate with the Wife of Bath. But nothing is farther from the essential truth. To insist that Molly's bluster is commensurate with her experience is rather like confusing locker room boasts with sexual prowess. What we have learned to detect in the latter is also true of the former: both come under that general heading known as "overcompensation."

Moreover, if we are what we read, Molly is a creature energized by cheap fiction and romantic distortions. Life can ever quite match *those* expectations: "its only the first time after that its just the ordinary do it and think no more about it why cant you kiss a man without going and marrying him first you sometimes love to wildly when you feel that way so nice all over you you cant help yourself I wish some man or other would take me sometime when hes there and kiss me in his arms theres nothing like a kiss long and hot down to your soul" (p. 740). In short, Molly prefers romantic kisses to phallic power, a statue of the boyish Narcissus to that "tremendous big red brute of a thing" (p. 742) she associates with Boylan. As Molly would have it, if men were all like the sun-naked boys who plunge into the Margate strand, "thered be some consolation for a woman" (p. 775). Besides, it is the non-threatening Narcissus—rather than erect, fully sexual men—who best approximates Molly's notion of "real beauty and poetry": "I often felt I wanted to kiss him [the statue of Narcissus] all over also his lovely young cock there so simply I wouldnt mind taking him in my mouth if nobody was looking as if it was asking you to suck it so clean and white he looked with his boyish face" (p. 776).

Whatever else Molly might be, she is certainly *not* a Joycean foreshadowing of Linda Lovelace. Molly's insistence that "a woman wants to be embraced 20 times a day almost to make her look young no matter by who so long as to be in love or loved by somebody" (p. 777) suggests affinities to that virginal temptress Bloom met in "Nausicaa." Gerty MacDowell reads the tripe of Miss Cummins rather than the pornography of Paul de Kock, but the differences seem more of degree than essential kind. Gerty, too, dreams of a man who would "take her in his sheltering arms, strain her to him in all the strength of his deep passionate nature and comfort her with a long long kiss" (pp. 351–52). In Gerty's case, however, the "ideal" man—complete with "hair slightly flecked with grey"—is a disguised version of the protective, providing father she does not have.

Molly is not only a good deal more experienced than Gerty, she is a good deal more interesting as well. Gerty is restricted to dreams of a husband who will shower her with adoring kisses and plans for a house beautiful without bedrooms. Molly knows better. But, even so, sexual passion is a hard disappointment. Kisses, on the other hand, become the ghosts which haunt her unsatisfying present. And that is doubly true of *first* kisses: Mulvey "was the first man kissed me under the Morrish wall my sweetheart when a boy it never entered my head what kissing meant till he put his tongue in my mouth was sweetlike young" (p. 759).

Interestingly enough, for all the differences of perception between Bloom and Molly (at one point in the novel Bloom will remember a night at the Gaiety when he tried, in vain, to discuss Spinoza with Molly; at another, Molly recalls that she began her period during the evening, while simultaneously flirting with "that gentleman of fashion staring down at me"), their accounts of the fateful kiss on Howth Head are nearly identical.

The moment on Howth Head *approaches* communion, but one made somewhat problematic by Molly's shifting pronoun referents. At times the "he" is Bloom on Howth Head; at times it is Mulvey under the Moorish wall. For Molly, it is the kiss itself which matters. Molly shares much of Gerty's romantic fascination with idealized love. Indeed, *all* the women of *Ulysses* represent avatars of Molly. Metempsychosis is not limited to the book's Homeric scaffolding; it operates within the internal structure as well. What Stephen insists upon in his *Hamlet* lecture also applies to Bloom and Molly: "We walk though ourselves, meeting robbers, ghosts, giants, old men, young men, wives, widows, brothers-in-love. But always meeting ourselves" (p. 213).

A final word: in a very real sense the interior lives of isolated people can *only* be a "ghoststory." *Ulysses* is not the sort of ghost story children ask for, complete with the gothic trappings of creaking doors and rustling sheets. Rather, it is the kind of story that results when the inner life is granted a full measure of the fictive canvas. Nor is it entirely coincidence that Ibsen, a writer Joyce especially admired, was also the author of a Modernist play entitled *Ghosts*. After all, if the artist really *is* a "god of creation" and *Ulysses* is Dublin frozen forever on 16 June 1904, one must resurrect the living as well as the dead, the hidden along with the revealed. Stephen could not forge such a story. Joyce did exactly that.

8

The Education of Vardaman Bundren in Faulkner's *As I Lay Dying*

LEE J. RICHMOND

THE CHILD as a central focus in the fiction of William Faulkner is most obvious in only two of his longer efforts—*Intruder in the Dust* and *The Reivers*—both lesser literary productions in the comparative sense. Children appear peripherally in each of his four major works—*Light in August, Absalom, Absalom!, As I Lay Dying,* and, most notably, *The Sound and the Fury*—where they shadow forth characters as adults. Like the minor novels mentioned, several key short stories revolve about children; the best include "The Bear" and "That Evening Sun." A large body of critical study has attended the readings of both full-length and short works. Surprisingly, no ambitious investigation has been attempted of the role of Vardaman Bundren, the youngest son of the beleagured clan in *As I Lay Dying*.

Of the fifty-nine sections of the novel—each is an interior monologue by either a Bundren or a friend or neighbor of the family—Vardaman is the narrative voice in ten. He is generally read, as he is by Irving Howe in his well-known study, as "perhaps deranged by the whole experience" of the journey to take Addie Bundren's corpse to Jefferson, as "pathetic and troubled," as a stock figure "borrowed from the common store of Southern fiction."[1] The earliest critical responses recognized a naive hill

1. *William Faulkner: A Critical Study* (New York: Vintage, 1952), p. 53.

people's primitive ethical duty to look properly after its dead, "in spite of constant temptation to abandon it, and in spite of multiplied difficulties put in [their] way by nature itself."[2] "The heroism of the effort" is seen in terms of a "promise or code" which leads to the continuance of a more stable existence after the "obligation" is removed.[3] In the matter of style, an astonishing effort is made to produce "an effect of the utmost reality and immediateness" in "fugue-like" manner through impressionistic technique.[4] General appraisals of this kind were made well into the fifties:

> It is important to recognize, also, that the effects of Faulkner's fragmentation of material are usually quite different from those produced by others who have used similar techniques. In works like *The Ring and the Book* and the Japanese film *Rashomon* various perspectives are thrown upon the same central event. In *Mrs. Dalloway* and *Ulysses* the seemingly unconnected experiences and events are occurring at the same time or on the same day. That is, either event, time or point of view is held constant. In *The Sound and the Fury, As I Lay Dying,* and *Absalom, Absalom!*, on the other hand, none of these is constant. The various narrators touch upon a few of the same events, but the selection of events seems determined essentially by the particular interests and obsessions of the narrator.[5]

For nearly three decades explicative criticism was scant and relatively cursory, until the appearance of Olga W. Vickery's prodigious effort.[6] Yet, for the many keen, insightful observations she gathered from *As I Lay Dying*, treatment of Vardaman still seems subject for further amplification. She suggests the boy is "too young to know what is happening," that with the maddened Darl

2. George Marion O'Donnell, "Faulkner's Mythology," *Kenyon Review* 1 (Summer 1939):290–91.
3. Robert Penn Warren, "William Faulkner," *New Republic* 26 (August 1946):234.
4. Conrad Aiken, "William Faulkner: The Novel as Form," *Atlantic Monthly* 164 (November 1939):653.
5. Walter J. Slatoff, "The Edge of Order: The Pattern of William Faulkner's Rhetoric," *Twentieth Century Literature* 3 (October 1957):115–16.
6. *The Novels of William Faulkner* (Baton Rouge: Louisiana State University Press, 1959); hereafter referred to in the text as *Novels*.

there is a "shared delusion" Addie is stirring in her coffin, and accordingly, "for both of them the world of fantasy has become as real as the concrete fact which we call reality" (*Novels*, p. 59). In sum, Vardaman's mind (largely attuned to sensory experiences and focused on information he collects while his mother is dying) is concerned, most emphatically, with "the meaning of death" (*Novels*, p. 62). His registrations of "tremendous shock," while not pointers toward derangement according to Vickery, are related to the question of mortality, which lead him to "a distorted conception of death" and, thus, make his actions "grotesque and incongruous" (*Novels*, p. 62). The critic's conclusion on Vardaman's characterization rests in the traumatizing effect of Addie's death: "Certainly Vardaman suffers from a delusion but an understandable one since it permits him to dissociate his mother from the horrors of physical death and decay: '*My mother is not in the box. My mother does not smell like that. My mother is a fish*'" (*Novels*, p. 62). Vickery's is a valid contention, but it does not round out Faulkner's splendid control when depicting other facets of Vardaman's role.

Later studies corroborate, in the main, Vickery's reading. Edmond L. Volpe's detailed discussions of the author's canon, for instance, largely reiterates Vickery's position: Vardaman is deeply "troubled by the death of his mother," suffers, in fact, "more psychological disturbance than anyone but Darl."[7] Recent criticism, less textual than general in presentation, ranges from the familiar to the overly ingenious in its handling of the boy. By orienting the novel around the figures of Addie and Darl and using "existential" analysis, Robert M. Slobey simplifies: "Although he is only a child, Vardaman shares the perplexity about the meaning of life that confronts Addie and Darl. Witnessing his mother's death has a terrible effect on him; everything suddenly becomes strange and unintelligible; and in his childish grief he becomes temporarily insane."[8]

Similarly, to Lewis Leary the boy, like Benjamin Compson,

7. *A Reader's Guide to William Faulkner* (New York: Noonday, 1964), pp. 130, 131.
8. "*As I Lay Dying* as an Existential Novel," *Bucknell Review* (December 1963):17.

reacts elementally to sensory impressions: "Nine-year-old Vardaman, who is torn by emotion, speaks only in images. All that he
knows of death is that fish die when taken out of water. His
mother, therefore, has become a fish."[9]

Finally, the value Robert R. Sanderlin attributes to Vardaman is circumscribed by a clustering of Christian symbols,
which, in no way suggestive of an "orthodoxly" Christian world-
view on Faulkner's part, provide thematic implications arising
from their presence in the novel: "Vardaman comes to symbolize
the devout believer. His childlike response of faith is for him a
means of handling the tragedies of life."[10] Vardaman's thoughts
about the fish and his mother suggest the Christian Eucharist. Because he refuses to believe Addie is dead and thinks he will see
her again, the boy is recalling symbolically the possibility of
Christian crucifixion and resurrection. Thus, "He is the one who
finds placation for the poignant realities of life and death by sub-
stituting a hope not borne out by the factualities of existence."[11]

Except for remarks of this kind, Vardaman is dismissed sum-
marily as a secondary character with small credibility. If this
impression is true, why then did the scrupulous craftsman
Faulkner include him in the complex pattern of As I Lay Dying?
Close textual analysis of Vardaman Bundren's role reveals a full-
bodied characterization and securely locates him in the author's
ambitious design.

At the immediate level, Vardaman's part constitutes a capsule
drama whose theme is the familiar one of coming of age. The
claustral world of the boy's mind is at odds with the teeming
world of effort and action evident throughout most of Faulkner's
folk tale-like narrative. As youngest child (significantly, he is the
last person Addie sees before her death), Vardaman comes to
stand for the inheritor of his family's—the adult world's—cogni-
tion of universal verities involved in the human condition:
violence, pain, deception, sexuality, good and evil, love and hate,
pity, the supernatural, social justice, nature's duality, and loss. In

9. William Faulkner of Yoknapatawpha County (New York: Crowell, 1973), pp.
69–70.
10. "As I Lay Dying: Christian Symbols and Thematic Implications," Southern
Quarterly 7 (October 1968):159.
11. Ibid., pp. 159–60.

a setting replete with death and tribulation, Vardaman is in his young manhood. His first mention comes in Tull's speech, where he is pictured carrying "a fish nigh long as he is," and spitting over his shoulder "like a man."[12] Tull reports that he cusses the fish "like a grown man" (p. 30). At once we see Vardaman swaggering onto the scene in imitation of his older brothers. While the other sons perform more taxing jobs about the farm, Vardaman contributes to the family's shaky stability by doing menial tasks, such as fishing. He is a boy, however, and when he tries to sneak away, Anse orders him to clean the fish, adding: "Well, I reckon I aint no call to expect no more of him than his mangrowed brothers" (p. 37). Anse's tone toward his older sons seems ironic in terms of his own laziness, but in any case Vardaman is emulating his brothers' masculinity. "Whew," he says in defense, "I'm pure tired." This focus is maintained later and more sharply when Vardaman joins forces in the struggle to get the coffin through the flood by holding onto the rope, "in that posture of rapt alertness" (pp. 150–51).

This, then, is one side of Vardaman, and it reflects a cursory inspection. Up to his first speech, he is mentioned sketchily in four other characters' monologs—Tull's, Peabody's, Anse's, and Darl's. The doctor tells only that Vardaman found the ploughline to pull him to the house (p. 41). Darl recounts the boy's peering at his dying mother's eyes: "She lies back and turns her head without so much as glancing at pa. She looks at Vardaman; her eyes, the life in them, rushing suddenly upon them; the two flames glare up for a steady instant. Then they go out" (p. 47).

We must return now to Vardaman's initial entrance. As he talks with Anse and Tull, "he looks down at the fish laying in the dust . . . and prods at the eye-bump with his toe" (p. 30). He picks it up, but it falls again, "hiding into the dust like it was ashamed of being dead, like it was in a hurry to get back hid again" (p. 30). Later, after cleaning the fish, Vardaman returns "bloody as a hog to his knees" (p. 37). Clearly, the fish is at first only an object of sustenance to the boy. Afterwards—and an en-

12. William Faulkner, *As I Lay Dying* (New York: Random House, 1964), p. 29. Subsequent references will be to this edition, and page numbers of excerpts are given parenthetically in the text.

tire section is made up of these five words—Vardaman says: "My mother is a fish" (p. 79). This is an instance of psychological transference. His speech makes this clear: "It is cut up into pieces of not-fish now, not-blood on my hands and overalls. Then it wasn't so. It hadn't happened then. And now she is getting so far ahead I cannot catch her" (p. 52).

Addie is dead when Vardaman says this, and in his mind the fish struggling to live and then dying becomes, through a surrealistic extension, his mother. Here is Vardaman's awareness of loss through mortality, and he reacts initially to it with a sense of futility and then a physical defiance. First, by saying, "And now she is getting so far ahead I cannot catch her," he associates the distance between life and death with the familiar physical action of running. Literally he does run crying to the stall, where he vomits from the shock of seeing someone die and from the rancid smell of fish on his fingers. Again, the two—fish and mother—are inseparable in his mind. Second, he reacts by unhitching Peabody's buggy. From the boy's innocent point of view, the doctor's appearance at the farm is the *cause* of Addie's death: "He kilt her. He kilt her" (p. 53). With childish defiance, he returns to the stall where he tells the cow: "I aint a-goin to milk you" (p. 54). His crying over, Vardaman says, "I am not crying now. I am not anything" (p. 55). There is a temporary feeling of dislocation which arises when he knows himself motherless. But, in the same breath, he thinks of the fish (and by association of his mother) as "an *is* different from my *is*." In other words, the fish is a body which does not have life, and is different from the boy's intrinsic knowledge of his own corporeality. He ends the speech: "I am not afraid." What, then, prompts him to run to Tull's house after this resolute determination? It is his third emphatic response to a growing sense of human mortality. Vardaman can only say initially, "You mind that ere fish." Later he adds, "The rain never come up till after I left. . . . I had done left. I was on the way. And so it was there in the dust. You seen it" (pp. 65–70). This is not so much derangement as it is a child's incredulity. Vardaman would like not to believe in Addie's death; in effect, he comes to Tull to plead with him to substantiate his disbelief.

The next morning Vardaman is found asleep by the coffin which he has bored full of holes with Cash's auger in an attempt to reach the corpse, as if to deny his mother's death (pp. 69–70). Hysterically, he had asked Cash before, "Are you going to nail her up in it, Cash? Cash? Cash?" (p. 62). And then he goes on quickly to tell how he got shut up in the dark crib where he couldn't breathe. He himself had experienced what he felt must be the sensation of being in a coffin. Since he is unwilling to accept truth at this traumatic point, he must think this is how Addie feels in the box. In the same speech his mind wanders from the preparation of the coffin to the model train and bananas which await him in Jefferson. This is a case of a child's selfish, even trivial want (although this selfishness is not to be construed necessarily as callousness) superseding something more important. Vardaman is concerned with something else here: why, because he is from the country and not the town, he should be deprived of things with which young boys find great delight. There is, in its most naive form, social awareness in his mind, and albeit in childish ignorance, a questioning of divine justice: " 'Why aint I a town boy, pa?' God made me" (p. 63).

In his next speech, Vardaman is talking with Darl. Darl says, "Jewel's mother is a horse." With pathetic ingenuousness, the younger son asks: "Then mine can be a fish, can't it, Darl?" If Jewel's mother is a horse, Vardaman goes on to say, his mother will have to be a horse, too. What follows, in dialectical form, is a strangely precocious discussion of ontology (pp. 94–96). Darl claims to have no mother which acknowledges his loss of a mother, and further implies a loss of identity—at least an identity that associates him with Jewel's mother. Darl is obsessed with consciousness, so much so that he neurotically disavows "the withness of the body": "I haven't got ere one [a mother]. . . . Because if I had one, it is *was*. And if it is was, it can't be is. Can it?" In Vardaman's desperate thinking, Addie has forfeited any claim she might have had as Darl's mother by her dying. Darl does concede, though, to Vardaman's claim that he is *are*. Darl: "That's why I am not *is*. *Are* is too many for one woman to foal." Half-mad with the idea that he is motherless because of Addie's excessive attentions toward Jewel, Darl cannot come to grips with the reality of his selfhood. Jewel's mother is not *his* mother. Darl is *are,* but he is not *is.* *Are* comes to mean nothingness, while *is* suggests connection with Addie or existence. Darl finally acknowledges: "I don't know what I am." Darl's irrational explanation does not seem to affect Vardaman. Vardaman says, "Pa shaves every day now because my mother is a fish." His incoherent thought-pattern is to be distinguished from Darl's, however, in that the boy's confusion is a condition of youth with its reluctant acceptance of what has to be. It is partly due, as well, to his "country boy" lack of sophistication. Further, Vardaman's statement may well reveal in a stream of consciousness manner an association of actions: Anse has shaved every day since Addie's death in anticipation of his neighbors' visits.

Part of the traditional "learning-story" is the discovery, however elemental, of moral values. Vardaman's "education" is not as roundly drawn as that of Isaac McCaslin in "The Bear" (which Faulkner himself called a "pageant-rite") or of Chick Mallison in *Intruder in the Dust* by virtue of the facts that both Ike and Chick are their stories' chief focal characters and both are more literate. However, Vardaman does make moral discoveries, even though they are presented with less dramatic charge. Two incidents especially relate to his moral growth. The first involves Vardaman only a little. It is the deception Jewel uses to reclaim his horse. Vardaman, like the others, joins in the hoodwinking of his father. This incident further underscores Addie's tyrannical rule of her children, with the youngest and most impressionable practicing the deceit she claims to abhor. The second and more detailed incident comes later in the action when MacGowan seduces Dewey Dell in the drug-store cellar. Vardaman sits outside, at Dewey Dell's request, until the light inside "winks out." With Vardaman's hyperimaginative sensibility, it is not improbable that he understands—if only intuitively—the evil going on in the darkened store. A cow enters the square—so Vardaman claims—and he says: "She had been in there a long time. And the cow is gone too. A long time. She has been there longer than the cow was. But not as long as empty." Earlier, after he had fled the house and hidden, Dewey found the boy and scolded him. He then told her he would not obey any orders; he would not, as was his custom, milk the cow. There is a connection here between the fecundity

of the milk-heavy cow and of Dewey Dell; for certainly, Vardaman is aware, if it is only a vaguely-felt awareness, of Dewey's
difference in sex, her femaleness. The image of the cow figures in
both scenes where Dewey and the boy are alone, and would
seem to be related to sexuality or fertility. This could be Vardaman's first awareness of the sexual relationships between human
beings. Moreover, it may be unfortunate for his moral growth that
this discovery involves an illicit and sordid meeting.

Vardaman, too, has something to report about the perilous attempt to get the coffin through flood waters. He recounts how
Darl unsuccessfully tried to "grabble" (a portmanteau word made
up of "grab" and "grapple") the floating box. Just like Vardaman's
fish, the coffin gets away. Again he makes a quick, childlike connection, more literal to his tender mind than metaphoric: "Where
is ma, Darl? . . . You never got her. You knew she is a fish" (p.
144). After recovering the coffin with concerted effort, the family
resumes its journey. Vardaman's next speech ponders where the
buzzards, which are circling the moving band, stay at night. "To-
night," he says, "I am going to see where they stay while we are
in the barn" (p. 201). The recurrent, horrific image of the buzzards is further indication of the boy's personal awareness of
death. It can signify also the duality of the natural world. Nature might be productive, but it is in equal measure predatory.
That the buzzards scent carrion would be part of Vardaman's
rural learning, but that they would feed on Addie's remains is a
fact that jars him into shocking recognition. It is while Vardaman is seeking the birds at night that he sees Darl set fire to the
barn in which the coffin rests.

Earlier, in another strange colloquy between Darl and Vardaman, the older son claims to hear Addie talking with God inside
the box. Vardaman, with a child's habit of wishful thinking, hears
her turn over on her side. She is alive for him, of course, because
he rejects her death. Darl, crazed, says she wants God to hide her
away from the sight of man, so she can lay down her life. Vardaman cannot comprehend this strange request, but as children do
accepts what elders say. With the wisdom of madness, Darl has
long intuited Addie's dissatisfaction in her life with Anse. Vardaman cannot be expected to grasp Darl's superhuman vision.

In the subsequent action, Vardaman learns more of the fragility of life when he asks Jewel about his burned back: "Does it hurt, Jewel?" (p. 214). With the awareness of death comes the knowledge and even acceptance of pain. He also sees the breakdown of Darl after the fire, and with a growing sense of imaginative sympathy comforts him: "You needn't to cry. . . . Jewel got out. You needn't to cry, Darl" (p. 215). Near journey's end, Darl says of Vardaman: "He too has lost flesh; like ours, his face has an expression strained, dreamy and gaunt" (p. 216). The trials by fire and water have forced Vardaman to see more of the severity and violence of life, as well as to act with the indomitable spirit of the others.

In his final monologue, Vardaman repeats Darl's name over and over. Darl has gone to Jefferson to the asylum for the insane: "My brother he went crazy." The sense of loss hits the boy hard. Another thing he once clung to has gone from his life. Through Faulkner's authorial prompting, we are strongly aware of Vardaman's sorrow and sympathy. His last word in the book is "Darl" (pp. 241–42). Vardaman and Cash are the only characters who express pity for their deranged brother. We can infer that Vardaman's feeling of privation is not entirely ego-centered, for he goes outside himself to a concern for a fellow being.

But Vardaman is not broken by the losses of mother and brother, or by the travails en route to Jefferson. In the concluding section we last hear of him with "mouth half open and half-et banana" in his hands, as Anse introduces the new Mrs. Bundren (p. 249). Vardaman has his bananas finally. Ironically, this is a kind of trivial reward for the hardships he has borne. We cannot expect him—nor the others, for that matter—to dwell long on the harsh details of death and journey. There is something in this family's spirit which is unbreakable and immutable. Vardaman, as youngest of the clan, develops the flexibilities which a human being needs to survive in the world of the living. This development is the nexus of his dramatic and thematic role in *As I Lay Dying*. In this regard, his is more than a journey to fulfill a dying mother's wish: it is a journey towards personal growth into a learning of loyalty, human suffering, and the acceptance of the difficulty of survival.

9

Hemingway and Revolution:
Mankinde Not Marx

JOSEPH M. DeFALCO

ERNEST HEMINGWAY's presentation of revolutions and revolutionary politics in his fictions from the mid-thirties to the beginning of World War II evoked from his critics responses that ranged from enthusiastic celebration to outraged condemnation. Most agreed that the artistic product was intimately involved with current political events, and not surprisingly the nature of the criticisms often reflected the preoccupations of the critics themselves. Those of the left, for example, were nearly of a mind that *To Have and Have Not* (1937) and *For Whom the Bell Tolls* (1940) presented crucial proletarian issues but failed to present a convincing portrait of solidarity within the masses. Too much individualism in the characterizations of Harry Morgan and Robert Jordan undermined what they saw as the overt tenor of these novels. The dedication of Philip Rawlings in *The Fifth Column* (1938) and his rejection of the bourgeois Dorothy Bridges was more palatable to the leftist critics, and they lauded Hemingway for his presentation of revolutionary idealism. Many of those who had doubted Hemingway's dedication to political idealism were firmly convinced of his sincerity with the production of the overtly propagandistic film, *The Spanish Earth*. Critics of other persuasions—middle-of-the-road, right, and apolitical—considered the play and the film alike as ill-conceived attempts to dramatize blatant propaganda. Similarly, the non-leftist critics had condemned *To Have and Have Not* as an overly self-conscious, proletarianized, lumping of dramatic segments. *For Whom the Bell Tolls* fared far better from all hands, but typically its failures were cited as "Not Spain But Hemingway."[1]

Perhaps in the political ethos of an Alvah Bessie in 1940, and even from the more moderate political perspective out of which Lionel Trilling was writing in 1941, the notion that Hemingway had deliberately politicized his fictional materials in order to achieve relevancy seemed a plausible explanation for the obvious shift in the treatment of his subject matter.[2] The leftists celebrated what they saw as a departure from the decadence of lost generation philosophy, but Trilling and others argued that the artist had surrendered to the man and what seemed a giving over of decadence was a giving in to artistic decline.[3] If the 1948 publication of *Across the River and Into the Trees* tended to confirm the latter view, the publication of *The Old Man and the Sea* convinced almost everyone that Hemingway's artistry remained intact.

With the advantage we have now of examining the writings of the second half of the thirties in the light of the major works which appeared after World War II, we can see the so-called political writings as productions of a middle period. As such, they reveal themselves as works of a transitional phase in Hemingway's underlying assumptions about human life and values. Regardless of the immediate stimulus, from the mid-thirties on Hemingway evolved out of his lost generation flirtation with nihilism and

1. Arturo Barea, "Not Spain but Hemingway," *Horizon* 3 (1941), reprinted in Carlos Baker, ed., *Hemingway and His Critics: An International Anthology* (New York: Hill and Wang, 1961), pp. 202–12. The above conclusions are my own, but see the detailed discussions of John A. Jones, "Hemingway: The Critics and the Public Legend," *The Western Humanities Review* 13 (1959):387–400, and Carlos Baker, *Hemingway: The Writer as Artist*, 4th ed. (Princeton, N.J.: Princeton University Press, 1972), pp. 237–45. See also the annotated entries in Audre Hanneman, *Ernest Hemingway: A Comprehensive Bibliography* (Princeton, N.J.: Princeton University Press, 1967).

2. Alvah Bessie, "Review of *For Whom the Bell Tolls*," *New Masses* 37 (1940), reprinted in Carlos Baker, *Ernest Hemingway: Critiques of Four Major Novels* (New York: Scribner's, 1962), pp. 90–94.

3. Lionel Trilling, "An American in Spain," *Partisan Review* 8 (1941), reprinted in Baker, *Critiques*, pp. 78–81.

moved toward a strongly humanistic and affirmative view of existence. When we compare the concerns which underlie the creation of a biologically trapped Jake Barnes in *The Sun Also Rises,* or the attitudes which went into the formulation of a despairing Frederic Henry in *A Farewell to Arms,* with that of the inspiration behind the creation of the larger-than-life Santiago of *The Old Man and the Sea,* the magnitude of the change in Hemingway's world view stands out in bold relief.

The age in which Hemingway wrote the works of the middle period may have demanded relevance and Hemingway may have attempted to answer that demand, but politicizing his fictions was the least important method he chose to meet that demand. As early as 1934, Hemingway had pointed out the danger to any writer's integrity who tried to use politics as a method of courting public applause: "don't let them suck you in to start writing about the proletariat, if you don't come from the proletariat, just to please the recently politically enlightened critics."[4] Perhaps Trilling and his followers would not agree that Hemingway took his own advice, but an examination of some of Hemingway's concerns that lie beyond the topical issues of the middle period suggests that he did.

The subjects of revolution and war which Hemingway engages in *To Have and Have Not* and *For Whom the Bell Tolls* provide a convenient means by which he achieves a surface realism, but other dimensions of the works argue for more profound considerations. The aphoristic force of the carefully crafted final statements of the protagonists demands that we read them as serious reflections of a theory of value. There is little qualitative difference between Harry Morgan's final view that "a man alone ain't got no bloody fucking chance" and Robert Jordan's "you can do nothing for yourself but perhaps you can do something for another,"[5] but the syllogistic progression charts the shift from self-concern to the concern for others. In *The Fifth Column,*

4. "Old Newsman Writes: A Letter from Cuba," *Esquire* 2 (1934), reprinted in William White, *By-Line Ernest Hemingway* (New York: Scribner's, 1967), p. 184.
5. *To Have and Have Not* (New York: Scribner's, 1937), p. 225; *For Whom the Bell Tolls* (New York: Scribner's, 1940), p. 466. Subsequent references are to these editions, and page numbers of excerpts are given parenthetically in the text.

Philip offers a like view when he tells Dorothy Bridges: "And where I go now I go alone, or with others who go there for the same reason I go."[6] One may read political sloganism into these final statements, but the characters have protested against just such a reading. For example, in *To Have and Have Not* Harry denies Albert's accusation that he is a radical, and Robert Jordan in *For Whom the Bell Tolls* declares that he is "without politics." Even Philip, who would seem more prone to political solutions, responds angrily to a soldier who addresses him as "Commissar": "I'm not a Commissar. I'm a policeman" (p. 18).

The protestations of the characters diminish considerably the extent to which the "curtain" remarks can be read as a reversal of Hemingway's often-cited hostility to abstraction and sentiment. Each is a product of a different fiction, however, and the density of the characterization in each instance affects the degree of thematic resonance achieved through these final statements. Even though *The Fifth Column* is a weak fiction, it does reveal the same shift toward a more comprehensive system of values. Although different demands are made upon Philip as a character, the difference in genre does not account for the limpness in his characterization. The failure lies in his lack of a meaningful conflict. What little inner conflict he does possess—the self as "fifth column," or enemy within—is presented mainly through the rather mild temptations of the seductive "Whore of Babylon" that Dorothy Bridges represents. His "I go alone" speech is less believable for this reason, but taken in conjunction with his actions in the course of the play his words emphasize a dedication to principles that anticipate Jordan's views.

If the episodic structure of *To Have and Have Not* is to blame for the lack of development of its major character and the consequent dilution of the social impact of his final words, there remains sufficient internal evidence to indicate that Hemingway attempted such a structure for sound artistic reasons.[7] Harry's conflict is limited by Hemingway because it is designed to be an

---

6. *The Fifth Column and Four Stories of the Spanish Civil War* (New York: Scribner's, 1969), p. 83. Subsequent references are to this edition, and page numbers of excerpts are give parenthetically in the text.

7. See Baker's account of the composition of the novel in *Hemingway*, pp. 203–205.

individual conflict. A significant part of the theme is revealed by
Harry's blind and quixotic battles against the oppressive forces of
the prevailing socio-economic system. Harry's final statement not
only moderates the naturalistic pathos of the novel's conclusion
but also indicates Harry's recognition that he has been fighting
the wrong battle all along. His refusal to accept defeat throughout the novel duplicates the feats of other "destroyed but unde-
feated" early Hemingway heroes, but to lump him with them is
to fail to see the evident shift that had taken place in Hemingway's world view. Harry recognizes the magnitude of the forces
that assail him, but he recognizes as well the necessity of aban-
doning the ways of self-interest. If Harry is left to die without passing on his insight, Hemingway's turn away from the "single combat" theme is clear.

It is no accident that Hemingway chose to echo Robert Burns
in the lines that he gives to Harry at a key juncture in *To Have
and Have Not:* "I'm sore. I been sore a long time," he tells Albert, "There's worse things than lose an arm. You've got two
arms and you've got two of something else. *And a man's still a
man* with one arm or with one of those" (pp. 96–97, italics
added). The lines from Burns's well-known poem, "For A'That
and A'That," are: "What though on hamely fare we dine, / Wear
hodden-gray, and a'that; / Gie fools their silks, and knaves their
wine, / *A man's a man for a'that*" (italics added).[8] Couched in
the American idiom, Harry's words convey the same outrage over
the victimization of the common man. Earlier, Harry had told
Albert: "My family is going to eat as long as anybody eats"
(p. 96). Harry's words are not simply revolutionary invective, as
we are reminded when he insists that he is not a radical. He responds in a primitive way to the threat of extinction, and his
words hint that he will return to his outlaw ways in the name of
survival. Nevertheless, Burns is the key to Hemingway's view.
Harry cannot see it, but the literary referent universalizes his
struggle and removes it from any immediate political context.
Hemingway's emphasis is Burnsian humanism and its assertion
of the significance and worth of the common man.

The humanistic emphasis does not drift into abstraction, for

8. Quoted from M. H. Abrams *et al.*, *The Norton Anthology of English Literature*
(New York: Norton, 1968), II: 40.

Harry's words echo in spirit those of Thomas Paine's *Rights of Man* as much as they do Burns's poem. It seems hardly debatable that Hemingway was not conscious of these echoes, nor would he have been unconscious of the effect these echoes would have upon his theme. If the Burns referent tends to universalize Harry's predicament, the Paine referent returns it squarely to the tradition of native American values. The thematic implications of the specific cultural referent can best be gauged by the movement implied between his early "a man's still a man" and his concluding "a man alone" statements. The call for brotherhood at the end can be read in Marxist terms, but the conflict throughout suggests the more general conflict of the individual's struggle for survival in an American culture grown hostile. The piratical Harry bears little resemblance to Burns's "honest man" because Hemingway conceives of Harry as a twentieth-century man forced by environmental pressures to revert to brute responses. Burns, on the other hand, conceives of his common man as a pastoral figure whose higher nature is suppressed by aristocratic exploitation. Hemingway's realism reflects a darker hue than Burns's softer satires because the stakes are larger. Harry's brutally primitive retaliations threaten the very premise upon which particular societies and all human culture is founded.

Hemingway illustrates the moral dimensions of Harry's actions in "Part One" when Harry offers a rationale for the killing of Mr. Sing and then condemns outright the same rationale when it is espoused by the Cuban revolutionary in "Part Three." Eddy asks Harry why he killed Mr. Sing, and the answer Harry gives reflects a simple ends-justify-the-means, pragmatic humanism: "To keep from killing twelve other chinks" (p. 55). Later, his private response to the Cuban's explanation that in revolutions "the end is worth the means" (p. 166) is a scathing indictment of the logic that allows for the destruction of individuals in the name of what amounts to an abstraction: "F— his revolution. To help the working man he robs a bank and kills that poor damned Albert that never did any harm. That's a working man he kills" (p. 168). Harry's insight here is a far-reaching one, for his ability to see the spurious logic of narrow-minded idealism leads him finally to see that his own views are equally destructive.

Harry's growing awareness that a means-ends pragmatism is essentially inhuman reveals itself as Hemingway chronicles Harry's responses to what might be termed "conch-hood." In the early part of the novel, Harry reveals his hatred for Mr. Sing's duplicity through understatement: "Some Mr. Sing"; later, he registers his disgust for the duplicity of Bee-lips even more vocally: "'Yeah. But this is here. This is where you were born. You know everybody that works there'" (p. 109). Just as Sing was willing to sacrifice twelve of his countrymen for money, so Bee-lips rationalizes his participation in the bank robbery that is to take place in his own community. Harry condemns both on the moral ground of his own changing ethic, for he sees the danger to all individuals in a community from such betrayals.

In the beginning, Harry had resisted the idea of conch-hood as a meaningful defense against oppression. As a "rummy" Eddy is the unlikliest of moral tutors, but he first expounds the theory of the fraternity of the conchs in "Part One" when he appeals to Harry's sense of loyalty: "Us conchs ought to stick together when we're in trouble" (p. 43). Since Harry plans to kill Eddy at this point, the question of loyalty to others of the same caste seems ludicrous. Hemingway crafts the scene in such a way, though, that Eddy is saved from death and Harry is saved from a vicious fratricide that would carry him beyond the point where moral growth could take place without violating verisimilitude. Later, in the liquor-running episode of "Part Two," Wesley questions Harry's sense of value: "Ain't a man's life worth more than a load of liquor" (p. 69)? Harry's recalcitrance elicits from Wesley an even more direct description of Harry's moral estate: "You ain't hardly human" (p. 69)! The near-killing of Eddy had already suggested the degree of Harry's imbrutement, and Wesley's words accentuate the degree to which Harry's cynical view of all human values have removed him from the community of his own kind. Only Captain Willie's selfless gesture moves Harry finally to a tacit acceptance of conch-hood. When he replies to Captain Willie's warning with "Thanks, brother," he begins the turn toward his final acceptance. Captain Willie's patronizing explanation to the bureaucrat from Washington defines conch-hood further in terms of one of the dominant images of the work: "Most everybody goes in boats calls each other brother" (p. 83).

The metaphor of conch-hood suggests an underlying humanistic postulate that informs the major themes of the work: the individual defines his humanity by actions which reflect his commitment to other individuals who comprise the social aggregate. Viewed in the context of the Great Depression setting and the correlative dramatizations of the feuding Gordons, the veterans from the government camp, and the decadent rich on their yachts, Harry's actions become part of the indictment of the causes of cultural atrophy. When Harry tells Albert that he has not been a conch "Since the first good meal that I ate" (p. 98), he reveals the rationale of self-interest that forces him to struggle in isolation in the nightmare that once was the American dream. Harry never realizes that the forces which oppress him are within as well as without.

Robert Jordan's discoveries in *For Whom the Bell Tolls* resemble those of his earlier counterparts in the play and novel, but the degree of insight into human values that Hemingway gives him is almost of a different order. Like Harry, Philip in *The Fifth Column* recognizes that the battles of life can be won only when the individuals in a society unite. Unlike Harry, Philip recognizes that such a unity can be achieved only under a single standard of shared values. Jordan commits himself to social action much as Philip does, but the resemblance ends there. In terms of political education and development, Jordan begins where Philip leaves off; in terms of human development and education, Jordan involves himself in the destiny of mankind in ways that would be inconceivable to Philip. Although Philip disavows party affiliations in the play, there is very little evidence to demonstrate that his motives are based upon anything other than some abstract equivalent. Jordan, on the other hand, comes to view society as a human organism rather than as a political mechanism. His experiences with the mountain bands brings him to an understanding that societal aggregates necessarily depend upon relationships that are fundamentally human.

What Hemingway worked out through the character of Robert Jordan dramatized what he had said in 1934: "it isn't all

in Marx nor in Engels, a lot of things have happened since then."⁹
As both an observer and participant in those "things" that go
beyond the pale of political theory, Jordan's transformation in
the novel catalogues the difference between political revolutions
and revolutions of the human spirit. Hemingway avoids the melo-
dramatic overtones of any sudden change in Jordan through a
carefully controlled narrative structure. Hemingway's heroes had
often been introspective, but none is more so than Jordan. Passages in which his sensibility in time present are judiciously inter-
woven with exposition presented through flashback reveal him
as something more than a political tyro. In the reflective segments, Jordan's private concerns mirror the complex social and
political issues of the Spanish war. Through the agency of Pablo's
band, Jordan discovers within himself strongly individualistic
tendencies and deep emotional needs that conflict with his commitment to act responsibly for the larger good represented by the
Republic. His eventual turn from that larger commitment allows
Hemingway to account for the impending failure of the political
revolution in Spain at the same time that he presents the necessary elements for a successful human revolution.

When Jordan is introduced into the novel, he is presented as
a prototypic political idealist. His willingness to go to any length
for the movement is remarked almost immediately: "He did not
give any importance to what happened to himself" (p. 4). This
is a partial disguise, however, and his businesslike and humorless
demeanor is deceptive. Although he is committed to his duty,
his year of political education has effectively annihilated his politics. As the succession of reflective segments reveals, Jordan is
well aware of the intrigue of the foreign intervenors and the
self-seeking divisiveness within the government of the Spanish
Republic. No longer is he the political innocent who had come
to Spain to fight "for all the poor in the world, against all tyranny,
for all the things that you believed and for the new world" (p.
236). Hemingway's strategy is revealed early when Jordan thinks
back to Golz and the orders given by him to dynamite the bridge.
As Jordan remarks later on to El Sordo, there is a difference be-

9. *By-Line Ernest Hemingway*, p. 181.

tween the giving of orders "on paper" and the execution of such orders. Paper orders suggest a mechanistic view of the control of individuals, but what Jordan discovers in the community of Pablo's band are human strengths and weaknesses that are of too much moment for him to continue to act in a detached way.

The cynicism that Golz expresses through the retrospective narrative parallels Jordan's growing disillusionment with the political machinations of the government leaders. The parallel extends further, for as foreigners both must organize and direct forces that have little or no cohesiveness. Although Jordan admires Golz, the difference between the two becomes evident through the attitudes that each holds toward their individual commitment and toward humanity in general. Golz works for "Madrid," the symbol of the ideal of a unified republic. Factionalism is the reality, however, and Golz is frustrated by its hindrance of an effective prosecution of the war. This same frustration is later attributed by Jordan to all of the Russians who congregate at Gaylords. Golz may be the wise old soldier, but his helplessness in the face of the ineptitude of those upon whom he must depend has effectively compromised his belief in the war. He suggests as much in his wry comment to Jordan: "I never think at all. Why should I? I am *Général Sovietique*. I never think. Do not try to trap me into thinking" (p. 8). After a year in the war, Jordan has convinced himself that he too must suspend "thinking" until the war is concluded. Hemingway makes it clear that Jordan's attempt to reserve judgment is doomed to failure, for he is too much of an individualist to accept unthinking regimentation and too much of an idealistic humanitarian to compromise his belief in the war. Hemingway calls our attention to these attitudes in Jordan when Jordan answers with some heat Golz's joking suggestion that he cut his hair: "'I have my hair cut as it needs it,' Robert Jordan said. He would be damned if he would have his head shaved like Golz" (p. 8).

The symbolism of hair in the novel has been noted on a number of occasions, but this early instance looks forward to its later more evocative association with Maria in ways that relate to Jordan's conflicting views. Jordan's Samson-like reluctance to cut his "sun-streaked fair hair" (p. 3) that contrasts with Golz's "shaven head crossed with wrinkles and scars" (p. 8) images Jordan as the inexperienced one. Hemingway even hints at a kind of virginal piety in Jordan's idealism through the answer Jordan gives to Golz's quiz about his relationship with women behind the lines: "No, there is no time for girls" (p. 7). The spoiled-unspoiled, virginal Maria puts the lie to this smug ideality in ways that go beyond the surface irony that emerges when he does fall in love. The imagery of Golz's shaven head and Jordan's uncut locks acquires additional valence through the story Maria tells of having her head shaved and being raped by the Civil Guard. As the center of that violence, Maria represents the despoilment of Spain itself. The shaven head imagery indicts both sides in the war as well as foreign intervention. Jordan remains unindicted through the imagery, for his uncut hair suggests the integrity of his commitment.

Hemingway transfers the religious aura of the name "Maria" to the character in his presentation of Maria as symbol, but finally he exploits that aura in a way that detaches the character from any formal religious significance. Aside from the more obvious ways that Maria and Jordan celebrate profane love, the symbolic construct of which both characters are a part is oriented toward the secular and human. Although Hemingway seems to urge a reading of Anselmo's partiality toward religion and Joaquin's sudden "conversion" in the heat of battle as indicators of a religious theme, the attacks made by various characters upon formal religion for its alliance with fascism, along with the constant underscoring of the superstitious nature of the peasant mind in the novel, suggests more that religion like politics enslaves the believer unless human values take precedence. Maria bridges ineffectual religious values and corrupt social values in a unique and secular way, and her literal credentials attest to her symbolic hybridism. In relating the details of the death of her parents at the hands of the Civil Guard, she tells Jordan: "My mother was an honorable woman and a good Catholic and they shot her with my father because of the politics of my father who was a Republican" (p. 350). Hemingway makes the point doubly when she relates further that she had planned to unite the final words of her mother and father and shout them in defiance of the enemy.

Unlike her father who had shouted "*Viva la República*" or her mother who was "not a Republican" and had shouted "*Viva* my husband," Maria intended to say, "*Viva la República y vivan mis padres*" (p. 350).

Love is the medium through which Maria finally brings about the transformation of Jordan. Hemingway invests the concept with a significance that suggests a religious experience, but he never allows a full-blown transcendental reading of the character's responses to its various manifestations. Pilar views it as mystical, but she is "superstitious." Maria sees it in the same way, but she is the offspring of both religious and secular parents. It is to Jordan that we must look for authorial suggestion. When he reflects upon the notion of "La Gloria," he defines it as analogous to native Spanish productions and works of Spanish masters which celebrate the ability of the human spirit to rise above the limitations of secular life. He hedges, however, and leaves it open to question: "I am no mystic, but to deny it is as ignorant as though you denied the telephone or that the earth revolves around the sun or that there are other planets than this" (p. 380). The elaboration in terms of technology and cosmograpy expands the implications vastly, but it does limit the comparison to an unknown but not unknowable finite realm. Jordan's experience leaves him with a sense of phenomenological wonderment not transcendental exaltation: "How little we know of what there is to know" (p. 380).

Jordan's early education in the movement had led him to a conversion that committed him to the "new world order." By the end of the novel, his love for Maria and his exposure to the influence of Pilar, his recognition of Pablo's nature, and his general acceptance by the band not only changes the implications of that commitment into a political cliché—as Gaylords had already done—but also rennovates his attitudes toward human existence. The sexual union with Maria achieves "La Gloria" in human terms, but as it parallels mystic annihilation of self, union with the "other," and transformation of the temporal into the eternal, it leads Jordan to the threshold of the principle upon which human order depends for all time. Hemingway never quite yields to sentimental optimism in presenting that principle, but he does allow the optimistic implications to emerge through the love banter of Jordan and Maria. For example, Jordan tells Maria that after the sex act they will be "one animal." Maria protests that they are "different," and then explains to Jordan: "It is better to be one and each one to be the one he is" (p. 263). The construct shams the Marxist dialectic by implying that the elemental formulation of a social aggregate from two "animals" who become a new "animal" while maintaining individual identity is biologically not historically centered. Love elevates mankind above other organisms when it is invoked as the dynamic of human aggregates, for it becomes the basis of a value system that is free of deterministic self-interest.

The gradual unfolding of Jordan's political skepticism is paralleled by his growing belief in humanity, and he reflects upon the ambitions of political leaders, the brutality of foreign intervention, and the misguided individualism that lies behind Spanish factionalism. Illuminated by the principle that Maria represents, the educational process that began with the Marxist piety of the International Brigade is no longer in danger of ending with the cynicism of Gaylords. Hemingway's world is not one where political organization based upon historical dialectics is the sole way a society may be constituted. The "Maria principle" indicates that love and compassion supersede all other modes. The Robert Jordan who is left alone and wounded to contemplate the nature of reality and the extent of an individual's responsibility to his kind has been transformed in the course of a novel from a cold, idealistic automaton to a warmly humanized member of the community that is summed up in Donne's "*Mankinde*."

Once Jordan comes in touch with the dynamic principle of human existence, that principle informs the stages of his transformation from dogged acceptance of an abstraction to an awareness of the necessity for shared values in all social actions. From the beginning of the novel, the inherent difficulty of accepting individual responsibility for the larger good is imaged by Jordan's role as dynamiter. The bridge is the central symbol around which much of the action revolves, but the packs which contain the dynamite elaborate the symbolic function of the bridge. As image, the dynamite in itself constitutes the tension between the opposing forces within the Republic. For those who give and follow orders issued in Madrid, the dynamite represents the instrument that will "win the war." To the guerrilla bands that reside in the hills, it represents the destruction of the factionalist "community" they have built for themselves and the consequent loss of security and comfort.

As Hemingway duplicates the larger social conflict through the mountain bands, he raises the question of the cultural issue involved. Pablo's band, for example, has done nothing for the loyalist cause since the Russian dynamiter was sent to blow up a train. As Pablo's concern with horses and the band's covert foraging from a cave suggests, the cultural level of the band has lapsed into a primitive stage barely distinguishable from that of the brutes. The high frequency with which the members of the band are associated with animals makes the point even more forcibly. Pablo's concern for the welfare of his own band and himself only reveals the slenderness of the bond which binds the mountain groups together as a "community." The larger social situation in the Republic is mirrored by the status of the bands and makes a telling comment upon social systems that depend upon imposed discipline rather than shared values.

From the first, the appearance in the narrative of the dynamite calls our attention to these larger issues. Initially, Jordan carries the pack with the dynamite while Anselmo assists with the other. As a middle-of-the-road Anarchist whose views border traditional Christianity, Anselmo is the first individual to whom Jordan gives any degree of trust in the sharing of the burden of the two packs. The true burden of the dynamite is Jordan's alone, and he reveals his reluctance to share that burden when he refuses Anselmo's offer to assist him in the shouldering of the pack. Later, when they meet Pablo, the bearing of the burden of the pack becomes the occasion for an altercation between Pablo and Anselmo. Pablo immediately recognizes the threat to his security that the dynamite represents, and in turn he poses the first immediate threat to Jordan's responsibility to carry out Golz's orders. As the pack-as-burden imagery is repeated throughout the novel, its metaphorical significance gains. Here, Pablo's initial denial but final acceptance of the burden foreshadows the broader pattern of his actions in the novel. He begins in sullen resistance, develops into an overt antagonist, and finally "converts" and accepts the necessity of the burden.

Pilar perceives the importance of the mission immediately and readily accepts the burden of leadership. Yet she is not equipped to assume the role. As the realistic Augustin points out to her when he argues that Pablo must be the one to lead the band from the mountains, neither Pilar nor Jordan have demonstrated the ability to assure the survival of the band. "Pablo, I *know* is smart" (p. 94), he tells Pilar. When Pilar is given the packs for safekeeping and fails to awaken while Pablo steals the exploder, Augustin's views are validated.

The shifting of the packs and the importance that Hemingway gives them in the overall metaphorical context is even more sharply revealed through Maria. As more and more details of her story are unveiled in the progress of the narrative, her function as symbol of hope for the survival of human values in Spain interweaves itself with the conflicting elements imaged by the dynamite pack. During the dynamiting of the train, Maria was saved by the members of the band at the risk of their lives. The dynamiting was essentially a "community" action, and the saving of Maria suggests the extent to which they were committed to a value system that had nothing to do with self-interest. The exchange with Joaquin at El Sordo's camp demonstrates the pride with which the act endowed the participants: "'I carried thee,' Joaquin told the girl. 'I carried thee over my shoulder.' 'As did many others,' Pilar said in a deep voice. 'Who didn't carry her'" (p. 131)? The exchange reflects as well the formula for social unity that Jordan learns from his intimacy with Maria. The youthful Joaquin emphasizes the role of individual action, but the wiser Pilar intrudes the more significant value of the act as a communal enterprise.

Jordan has a direct insight into the figurative roles that Pilar, Maria, and Joaquin play as representatives of a human morphology. As he watches them walking, he formulates a metaphor that suggests the continuity and renewal of human life in nature: "You could not get three better-looking products of Spain than those. She is like a mountain and the boy and girl are like young

trees. The old trees are cut down and the young trees are growing clean like that" (p. 136). When Pilar allows Jordan to take
Maria, the figurative significance of the act takes its meaning
from what Jordan has observed. Pilar has passed the burden of
the hopes and ideals of the new Spain into his keeping. The two
burdens intersect at this point, and Jordan must juggle his responsibilities to Golz's orders and his responsibilities to what
Maria has come to represent. Since Maria's love has brought him
into the sphere of communal influence in a way that he has not
experienced before, his desperate attempt to get a message to
Golz in order to save the band is all the more futile. If he now
savors life where before it was of little importance, the attempt
to preserve it through an appeal to that authority which has
misled him all along marks the final failure of its power to restore
order out of the chaos.

The appeal to a mute authority and its inability to respond
generates a context that gives meaning to Jordan's "martyrdom"
at the conclusion of the novel. The politics of Madrid is so far
removed from the people it claims to serve that it cannot respond
to the human needs of the individuals who must give their loyalty
to the larger aggregate before it can survive. On a different
level, Jordan understands the need for the smaller aggregates to
survive. Pablo's social horizons may be limited, but his alienation
from the band and his "conversion" to the joys of social harmony
emphasize Jordan's own conversion. Survival comes to mean
something more than physical existence, and Pablo makes this
clear when he returns to the band: "I do not like to be alone.
Sabes? Yesterday all day alone working for the good of all I was
not lonely. But last night. *Hombre! Que mal lo pase!*" (p. 391).
Jordan's progress from alienation and disaffection to acceptance of
his kind and insight into a new order of social solidarity is capped
by his final act. His acceptance of Pablo and Pablo's acceptance
of him restores the imbalance created by Jordan when he entered
the hills with the dynamite. If the literal destruction of the bridge
proved to be of no military value, the willingness of Pablo and
the band to share the burden which the dynamite represents suggests the hope for the future of society. Pablo seems to be the
victor at the conclusion of the novel not because his narrow

horizons and brutish actions are best; rather, his ways are the only possible ones under conditions that threaten survival.

Jordan's self-sacrifice provides the counter to the reality that Pablo's final supremacy represents. Jordan passes the burden of Maria into Pablo's hands because that is the only way that her survival can be insured. His own final gesture, however, is the more significant action in terms of Hemingway's thematic emphasis upon the pre-conditions necessary before a society can exist and finally prosper. Reality for Hemingway does not necessarily favor good intentions, but Jordan's view that "perhaps you can do something for another" gives his act of "holding on" the character of martyrdom. It is this kind of act that is the truly revolutionary act in Hemingway's humanism. After Robert Jordan, the Hemingway hero is no longer fettered by the egocentrism that marked many of the early heroes. Jordan's final actions are meaningful in the way they depict the supreme act of altruism. Jordan does not die for duty to the Republic. He dies to insure the survival of the community that he had joined and to insure the continuity of that identity it had given him.

10

Ineffability in the Fiction of
Jean Toomer and Katherine Mansfield

WILLIAM RANKIN

THERE ARE SURPRISING SIMILARITIES in the fictions of Jean Toomer and Katherine Mansfield, two contemporary writers from literary situations far removed from one another. Both writers share a common concern with ineffability and seem to be moving to a point of near renunciation of language. There is a like despair before the impossibility of precisely capturing emotions, feelings, and states of mind.

Mansfield's and Toomer's stories usually cannot quite be told—the immediate impression is that they attempt to communicate something inexpressible. The tales often center about an unfathomable symbol or mystery, a passion that is beyond words, an intense but elusive experience. A character's relationship with other characters, his relationship to life, his confrontation of self are at the core of many of the stories.

Toomer's "Avey" and Mansfield's "Psychology" give us two clear examples of the problems in human relatonships. In "Avey" the narrator's feeling for the title character can be expressed only in negative terms: "I could feel by the touch of it, that it wasn't a man-to-woman love. . . . I didn't know what it was, but I did know that I couldn't handle it."[1] Indeed, Avey's "own nature and

1. Jean Toomer, *Cane* (New York: Liveright, 1951), p. 43. Subsequent references are to this edition, and page numbers of excerpts are given parenthetically in the text.

temperment" are described as needing "a larger life for their expression" (p. 46). Similarly, the "he" and "she" of Mansfield's "Psychology" suffer from uncertainty about a relationship that is not quite passion, not quite something else. Their conversation is interrupted constantly by enigmatic silences: "They faltered, wavered, broke down, were silent. Again, they were—two hunters, bending over their fire, but hearing suddenly from the jungle beyond a shake of wind and a loud, questioning cry."[2] Later in the story, when "she" receives a lady friend, we see another disturbing situation, and the protagonist feels "the silence that was like a question." Silence is used as a symbol for the enigmatic and evanescent quality in human relationships.

In Toomer and Mansfield the relationship between a character and life itself can be vague and ineffable. Mansfield's "The Daughters of the Late Colonel" and "Life of Ma Parker," and Toomer's "Esther" are good examples. Here are stories of people who have no hold on life, no apparent place in it, and no way of expressing themselves. Constantia, for example, in "The Daughters of the Late Colonel," is aware of something she is missing, something she feels and does not quite understand. She regards the miniature Buddha on her mantlepiece which "seemed to-day to be more than smiling. He knew something; he had a secret. 'I know something that you don't know,' said her Buddha. Oh, what was it, what could it be? And yet she had always felt there was . . . something" (p. 282). A later reflection brings her close to an insight about the isolated and unreal quality of her past life: "it all seems to have happened in a kind of tunnel. It wasn't real. It was only when she came out of the tunnel into the moonlight or by the sea or into a thunderstorm that she really felt herself. What did it all lead to? Now? Now?" (p. 284).

Toomer's Esther, the youthful dictie shopkeeper in a southern American town, lives with the same dreamy perception of her life as do the elderly maiden daughters of the late Colonel. Toomer describes her as having "a vague sense of life slipping by," and compares her to a somnambulist. Her attempt to engage life by offering herself to the drunken and sensual Barlow fails as

2. Katherine Mansfield, *Collected Stories of Katherine Mansfield* (London: Constable and Company Ltd., 1956), p. 80. Subsequent references are to this edition, and page numbers of excerpts are given parenthetically in the text.

she is unable to accept her action, and the story concludes with
Esther metaphorically isolated: "She steps out. There is no air, no
street, and the town has completely disappeared" (p. 25). Mansfield's Ma Parker, an elderly cleaning lady who has lost her grand-
child, her only real tie with life, has no place to go and weep.
One sees, however, that it is not so much the *place* to express
grief which is lacking but, more profoundly, the very *possibility*
of expressing it. The concluding lines of the story resemble those
of "Esther": "Oh, wasn't there anywhere where she could hide
and keep herself to herself. . . . Wasn't there anywhere in the
world where she could cry out—at last? Ma Parker stood, looking
up and down. . . . There was nowhere" (pp. 308–309).

Ineffability is also to be found in Toomer's story "Fern." Fern
is unable to have meaningful relationships with anyone. Though
she is presented as promiscuous, yielding to and greatly desired by
men, she is described by Toomer as *becoming* a virgin, so unreal
is even her sexual contact. Her engagement with the world around
her is similarly vague; she is part of it and yet not part of it.
Toomer's description of her from the point of view of the narrator points this up: "eyes vaguely focused on the sunset. Saw her
face flow into them, the countryside and something that I call
God, flowing into them. . . . Nothing ever really happened.
Nothing ever came to Fern, not even I. Something I would do
for her. Some fine unnamed thing" (p. 17). Nevertheless, Toomer
makes it clear that Fern has an urgent need for expression: "Her
body was tortured with something it could not let out. Like boil-
ing sap it flooded arms and fingers till she shook them as if they
burned her. It found her throat, and spattered inarticulately in
plaintive, convulsive sounds, mingles with calls to Christ Jesus.
And then she sang, brokenly. A Jewish cantor singing with a
broken voice. A child's voice, uncertain, or an old man's" (p. 17).

A like musical symbol appears in Mansfield's "Honeymoon":

It [the band] began to play again. Something boisterous, reckless,
full of fire, full of passion, was tossed into the air, was tossed to
that quiet figure [a tall old man with white hair], which clasped
its hands, and still with that far-away look, began to sing. . . .
Nothing was heard except a thin, faint voice, the memory of a

voice singing something in Spanish. It wavered, beat on, touched the high notes, fell again, seemed to implore, to entreat, to beg for something, and then the tune changed, and it was resigned, it bowed down, it knew it was denied   (p. 406–407).

The song stands for the expression of the deeper self in Toomer and Mansfield. It may be, as in the cases cited, fully described or simply alluded to, as in Mansfield's unfinished "A Married Man's Story": "I looked at the dead bird . . . and that is the first time that I remember singing—rather . . . listening to a silent voice inside a little cage that was me" (p. 443). A more elaborate description of the married man's inner state occurs later when Mansfield uses another of her recurrent symbols of the deeper self: "A feeling of awful dreariness fastened on me. . . . I felt so strangely that I couldn't move. Something bound me there by the table. . . . Then the shrivelled case of the bud split and fell, the plant in the cupboard came into flower. 'Who am I?' I thought. 'What is all this?' " (pp. 446–47). Another use of flower symbolism occurs during the ruminations of the lonely woman in Mansfield's "Late at Night": "I want to show them—even give them a hint—that I like them, they seem to get frightened and begin to disappear. . . . I am sure that most women don't have this tremendous yearning to express themselves. I suppose that's it—to come to flower almost. I'm all folded and shut away in the dark and nobody cares" (p. 649).

In "Kabnis" Toomer gives us a symbolic personification of thwarted expression and the consequent thwarted development of personality in the character of Father John, the embodiment in extreme form of the problem of the Negro in the South. He is described as "A mute John the Baptist of a new religion—or a tongue-tied shadow of an old. . . . Dead, blind father of a muted folk who feel their way upward to a life that crushes or absorbs them" (pp. 104–105). The author intrudes here for a moment, begging Father John to speak: "Speak Father!" But Father John does not speak throughout the novella, except at the end where he painfully and with difficulty utters a brief sentence which appears obvious and self-evident. As with Ma Parker, the feeling seems too intense for expression.

Another symbolic figure in "Kabnis" is the titular character who believes himself an orator, though most of his orations are interior monologues. He, too, cannot adequately express himself. He, however, is Toomer's most eloquent articulator of the problem of expression: "People make noise. They are afraid of silence" (p. 84). But Kabnis himself finds no audience to listen: "Who in Christ's world can I talk to? A hen. God. Myself . . ." (p. 85). Nevertheless, his mind is at work constantly on the problem of expressing his deeper self: "I've been shapin words t fit m soul" (p. 109). Lewis, Kabnis' alter ego, discusses Kabnis as follows: "Life has already told him more than he is capable of knowing. It has given him an excess of what he can receive" (p. 99). Acceptance and expression of what one feels and knows appear the conditions of vital living, but acceptance and expression seem impossible.

What is the meaning of Mansfield's and Toomer's concern with the ineffable, with something that must but apparently cannot be expressed? Both writers want to describe a kind of mystical experience or, put differently, to render "pure" experience. The state they wish to describe is not one of a special grace bestowed upon a religious elite, but a deep relationship with self and with life open to every person. The problem, as they see it, is not to have the experience, but to be able to accept, understand, and articulate it. Their characters respond with varying degrees of refusal, suffering, and acceptance; some fail in the face of the experience, while others seem to transcend it.

In "Miss Brill," Mansfield presents a case of failure. Miss Brill, an aging schoolteacher lacking understanding or acceptance of the darker side of life, fantasizes herself an actress, just as Toomer's Kabnis sees himself an orator. Attending a Sunday band concert, Miss Brill feels herself a performer on the stage and, at the same time, has a deep experience of life: "The band . . . started again. And what they played was warm, sunny, yet there was just a faint chill,—a something, what was it?—not sadness— no, not sadness—a something that made you want to sing. The tune lifted, lifted, the light shone; and it seemed to Miss Brill that in another moment all of them, all the whole company would begin singing" (p. 334–35). Miss Brill falls into the trap of a facile and sentimental euphoria which is shattered when she overhears a young couple discussing her. It is apparent from the beginning of the story that Miss Brill is inclined to a prejudiced and even scornful view of the people she sees in the park. She likes only what is young and beautiful, and she is disillusioned when she discovers the two young lovers view her in the same critical way that she views others.

The case of Miss Brill contrasts with that of the narrator of "The Canary," an elderly woman quite capable of understanding that her young boarders laugh at her and call her a scarecrow. She is able even to laugh over it with her canary. When the canary dies, her response to the death of the bird makes us see what is universal in the relationship among all living things.

The most direct presentation of mystical aspiration in Mansfield's fiction is in the story "Escape." As the title suggests, we find here a solution to the problems of isolation and imprisonment suggested throughout Mansfield's work. Words such as *tunnel, cage, bound, cupboard, shut-off* abound. The patient husband of the self-pitying termagant, who is sent away as a kind of punishment for her own ill-humor, has an intense experience of liberation and fulfillment:

> He felt himself, lying there, a hollow man, a parched, withered man, as it were, of ashes. . . . It was then that he saw the tree, that he was conscious of its presence just inside a garden gate. It was an immense tree with a round, thick silver stem and a great arc of copper leaves that gave back the light and yet were sombre. . . . As he looked at the tree he felt his breathing die away and he became part of the silence. It seemed to grow, it seemed to expand in the quivering heat until the great carved leaves hid the sky, and yet it was motionless. Then from within its depths or from beyond there came the sound of a woman's voice. A woman was singing. The warm untroubled voice floated upon the air, and it was all part of the silence as he was part of it. Suddenly, as the voice rose, soft, dreaming, gentle, he knew that it would come floating to him from the hidden leaves and his peace was shattered. What was happening to him? Something stirred in his breast. Something dark, something unbearable and dreadful pushed in his bosom, and like a great weed it floated, rocked. . . . Deep,

deep, he sank into the silence, staring at the tree and waiting for the voice that came floating, falling, until he felt himself enfolded.
(pp. 201–202)

By comparing this experience with Miss Brill's we can see its greater scope and authenticity. The husband seems willing to accept the extremes of joy and horror in life. This passage combines two types of mystical experiences: ecstasy and illumination on the one hand, and the "dark night of the soul" on the other. In these lines we can find many examples of what might be called "mystical vocabulary." Included are words suggesting mystery, like *sombre, hidden, dark, floating, falling;* words implying negation, like *hollow, withered, ashes, unbearable, dreadful;* and words hinting at mystical union, like *presence* of the tree, *grow expand, singing, all part of the silence, peace,* and *enfolded.* We find this same vocabulary elsewhere in the work of Mansfield. The words related to the experience are most frequently *tree, flower, wind, sea, bird.* There is also a high preponderance of negative diction, such words as *nothing, nowhere, empty, blankness, could not remember.* The recurring question in story after story—"What is it?"—is often followed by a searching but usually unsuccessful attempt to bring to focus an ineffable "something."

In the above passage we also find a device more typically Toomeresque—an insistent use of contradictions. Singing is described as part of silence, expansion as part of motionlessness. Toomer most frequently expresses ineffability by striking such contradictory juxtapositions:

Kabnis wants to hear the story of Mame Larkins. He does not want to hear it.

Dan I could love you if I tried. I don't have to try. I do. . . . What has she got to do with me? She *is* me, somehow. No she's not. Yes she is.

Upsets me. I am not upset.

I bet he can love. Hell he cant love. . . . He wouldn't love me anyway. . . . Maybe he would. Maybe he'd love.

Come where? Into life? Yes. No. Into the crimson gardens.

These and many subtler examples can be found throughout *Cane,* and this technique is most noticeable in the second section of the book.

The opposition of song and silence also fascinates Toomer as well as Mansfield. Stories end or begin with song or silence. This opposition suggests ineffability since both song and silence are, in a sense, beyond language, and yet represent a kind of ideal mystical expression.

The major literary weapon for expressing the unexpressable is metaphor. Thus, external action is notably unimportant in Toomer's and Mansfield's works; frequently metaphor seems to take the place of plot. Even where we find a conventional "plot," as in Toomer's "Blood Burning Moon," the action itself is transformed into metaphor or symbol. In Mansfield, the action is often insignificant as action. Our attention is directed to the symbolic significance of minute occurrences. What stands out particularly in both writers is the use of microcosmic-macrocosmic associations in a way that recalls the metaphysical poets of the seventeenth century. A glance at Mansfield's typical titles—"Sixpence," "The Doll's House," "A Cup of Tea," "The Fly," "The Canary," "The Dove's Nest," "A Dill Pickle" testifies to her love of the miniature and microcosmic. But a perusual of these stories reveals the presence of the large as well. Two beds appear to be two ships, lightning flutters like a broken bird trying to fly, flickering candles are stars, oranges are little worlds of burning light, a brass gong burns like a fallen sun in a dark hall, and the little lamp in "The Doll's House" corresponds to reality. In "The Canary," the narrator's affection fixes first upon flowers, then upon a star, then upon a canary. The use of extremes can be found noted in Mansfield's *Journal* for November 1906, in what appears to be the earliest presentation of the experience which seems at the core of her vision:

Like the great white bird the ship sped onward—onward into the unknown. Through the darkness the stars shown; yet the sky was a garden of golden flowers, heavy with colour. I lay on the deck of the vessel . . . and watching them I felt a curious complex emotion—a swift realization that they were shining steadily . . . into the very soul of my soul. I felt their still light permeating the very depths, and fear and ecstasy held me still—shuddering. . . . As the power of sunlight causes the firelight to become pale and wasted, so is the flame of my life becoming quenched by this star—shining. I saw the flame of my life as a little, little candle flickering fearfully and fancifully, and I thought before long it will go out; and then even as I thought I saw there where it had shown darkness remained. Then I was drifting, drifting—where, whence, whither? I was drifting in a great boundless purple sea. . . . I knew this sea was eternal.[3]

In this passage we find a juxtaposition of the small and the large, the intimate and the universal: "bird" and "ship," "stars" and "soul," "sunlight" and "firelight," "flame of my life" and "star-shining," "flame of my life" and "little, little candle," "sea was eternal" and I was eternal. Mansfield's reliance on metaphoric techniques, so evident here, is very characteristic, and is exploited further in such prose poems as "Bank Holiday" and "Spring Pictures."

The poetic orientation of Toomer is a secret to no one. Some of the more extreme examples of microcosmic-macrocosmic association include white paint on houses compared to the glitter of distant stars, a woman's skin compared to dusk on the eastern horizon, a man seen as an atom of dust in agony on a hillside. There are other even more striking examples: "The body of the world is bull-necked. A dream is a soft face that fits uncertainly upon it." The imagery is striking in poems such as "Storm Ending" which opens: "Thunder blossoms gorgeously above our heads, / Great, hollow, bell-like flowers." In "Beehive," where the city is seen as a black hive swarming with a million bees, we have a remarkable microcosmic-macrocosmic association: "Earth is a waxen cell of the world comb."

3. J. Middleton Murry, ed., *Journal of Katherine Mansfield* (London: Constable & Company Ltd., 1954), p. 5.

The entire structure and meaning of *Cane* is centered around métaphor. The book begins with a girl whose skin is compared to dusk and ends with a highly developed dawn image, where the sun is metaphorically a child: "Outside, the sun arises from its cradle in the tree-tops of the forest. Shadows of pines are dreams the sun shakes from its eyes. The sun arises. Gold-glowing child, it steps into the sky and sends a birth-song slanting down gray dust streets and sleepy windows of the southern town." We have been prepared for this extraordinary image earlier by Toomer's evocative suggestion that "Night winds are the breathing of the unborn child whose calm throbbing in the belly of a Negress sets them somnolently singing." It is chiefly through the closing metaphor of birth and hope that we sense the mystical vision behind the somber surface of *Cane*.

Throughout the work of Mansfield and Toomer the polarities of union and separation are stressed. Relationships oscillate between extremes of isolation and union. The core of Kabnis' prayer is: "Dear Jesus, do not chain me to myself." The most memorable symbol of isolation is Becky, the poor southern white living alone in a little shack on a narrow island of land between railroad and road and ignored by everyone. Union, on the other hand, is experienced by John in "Theater," where he feels "as if his own body were the mass-heart of a black audience" (p. 50). The experience is further amplified: "The walls awake. . . . The walls sing and press inward. They press the men and girls, they press John toward the center of physical ecstasy" (pp. 50–51). The most ample expression of mystical aspiration to union is to be found in Toomer's later poem "Blue Meridian."

Many of Mansfield's characters are solitary or feel they are hidden away, forgotten, in cupboards, cages, caves, or tunnels. Old Mr. Neave, for example, in "An Ideal Family," sees himself as a lonely spider climbing up and down endless stairways. But characters have moments of unity as well, like the brother and sister of "The Wind Blows," who "stride like one eager person through the town." An experience of union much like the one in Toomer's "Theater" happens to the narrator of "This Flower": "Could she describe what happened? Impossible. It was as though . . . she was part of her room—part of the great bouquet of southern anemones, of the white net curtains that blew in stiff against the light breeze, of the . . . quivering clamour . . . and crying voices that went streaming by outside—part of the leaves and the light" (p. 672).

The differences between Toomer and Mansfield are immediately apparent. Perhaps the most obvious is that while Mansfield strikes the reader as disarmingly simple, light, and perhaps even sentimental, as being a popular and perhaps not too intellectual writer, Toomer appears sophisticated, experimental, and even hermetic. However, the more one reads and compares these writers, the more one becomes aware of the restless experimentation and extraordinarily elaborate symbolic unity of Mansfield's stories and the underlying simplicity and clarity of Toomer's vision. Both writers are distinguished by their highly poetic use of metaphor and the way in which their stories, prose poems, and poems illuminate each other. Each narrative appears as a fragment of a rich kaleidoscope of vision aimed at communicating an intuition of reality, a common experience constantly changing in tone, constantly seen from a new perspective.

It seems not an insignificant coincidence that in the early 1920s both Toomer and Mansfield arrived at the Gurdjieff Institute at Fontainbleau, France. The goal of achieving an awareness of the deeper self, of progressing to a special world or, put another way, "cosmic consciousness" is implicit, as we have seen, in much of their work. The Gurdjieffian method of constant alternation of social roles, from servant to gardener, cook, artist, director, manual worker, intellectual, is what Toomer had been trying to do with his fictional probing of the southern white, northern white, poor southern black, dictie, northern intellectual, prostitute, carpenter, poet. This method is also reflected in Mansfield's diverse characters, a cleaning woman, pretentious Bohemian French writer, governess, wealthy society women, Bloomsbury intellectual, valetudinarian, patient husband, forgotten grandfather. All of the characters long for a deeper understanding of themselves and life, and for a way to express it.

The seeming ineffability of life was the challenge that stirred Toomer and Mansfield to attempt to find words. Though their writing frequently deals with brief moments, microcosmic in nature, these moments appear to capture within them reflections of the larger universe. Their work has vibrance and intensity because of their tendency to paint a highly personal experience in terms of a universal one. The universal represents any person's, or for that matter any creature's, confrontation with reality and with the mystery of life. Few writers are as possessed by the strong compulsion to express what they feel so surely cannot be expressed. This mystical quality which underlies the work of Mansfield and Toomer gives them passionate humility before the word and before those for whom they write.

11

The Art of Glenway Wescott

Alfred Kolb

G LENWAY WESCOTT's earliest work of fiction, *The Apple of the Eye*, has never won the critical acclaim of *The Grandmothers* or *The Pilgrim Hawk* despite its simplicity, engaging autobiographical detail, and special combination of art and craft which allows highly personal literary recollection to become mythopoeia. Indeed, Wescott's use of personal experience and private memories as a springboard to shared experience is his *métier*. As he notes in *Images of Truth:* "Evidently everything is connected and involved in fact. We learn to think almost entirely in contrasts and juxtapositions, in the famous antinomies: good and evil, land and sea, day and dark, art and ignorance. It probably is the right way to think. . . . Those contrasts and antitheses are basic to literary art. What we call the creative spirit really does not create anything. It evokes and recollects and relates."[1]

One of Wescott's artistic techniques is to allow the past to impinge upon the present and, through the shape, color, and texture of language, create a special moment in time. In *The Grandmothers* he achieves this through the dreams and memories of Alwyn Tower, the last scion of a typical midwestern pioneer family. With the aid of the old family photo album, Alwyn, who lives abroad, retells the family chronicle; he relates it not only

1. Glenway Wescott, *Images of Truth: Remembrances and Criticisms* (New York: Harper and Row, 1964), p. 10.

for those people, events, and ideas he left behind in America, but also in order to define himself and his own place in that very chronicle. But Wescott's concern with family and folk memories, with mothers and fathers who, though dead physically, are spiritually alive in the minds and hearts of their children, this concern is not confined solely to his fiction. The technique informs his critical evaluations also.

> Indeed, we fiction writers question everyone and make what we can of the answers. We rouse up our own memories, experience scarcely worth remembering, time that has gone to waste all our lives; but it is not because we love the past, it is because we fear the future. It is not in self-love but to save ourselves, and others as well, if we are good at it. We raise the dead and we make them speak; but for those of us who are true novelists it is not as a means of expressing our particular opinion. We ask the dead questions and pass the information on. We do not simply utter our experience through them. They are not puppets, they have voices of their own; and the heart of every matter as we see it seems to come to us from their knowledge, as it were independent of our knowledge, prior to our experience. . . . Death: It is an untying of the nerves, so that the flesh and the bones and the psyche disperse, dissociate. This beautifully exemplifies in minature our fiction of remembrance and reawakened, recalled emotion.[2]

These sentiments, then, should guide us in the examination of *The Apple of the Eye,* a book whose very title points up the dichotomy and tension between various ethical, sexual, and religious choices.[3] On one level the story is a typical maturation tale, a kind of *Bildungsroman;* it is the tale of Daniel (in the lion's den) Strane (straining for identity, uniqueness, the last strain of the family's line). The narrative covers his journey from innocence to experience, from boyhood to manhood, from small midwestern town to metropolis. But it is not entirely Dan's story, at least not at the outset. It is also the story of all those forces,

---

2. *Ibid.,* pp. 17–18.
3. See King James Version of the *Old and New Testaments* (New York: World, 1967), p. 526 (*Proverbs* vii, 2).

events, and ideas which ultimately affect and shape his character
and outlook, drawing him forth into the larger world. In that re-
spect the book's pattern, in keeping with the epigrammatic excerpts from Bunyan's *The Pilgrim's Progress,* Defoe's *The Fortunate Mistress,* and Sterne's *Tristam Shandy,* which alert the reader
to the fact that the book lends itself to wider interpretation, anticipates that of *The Grandmothers.*

Wescott subdivides *The Apple of the Eye* into three books,
each carrying the name of the character whose story it holds. Although the stories are told from the character's point of view, they
are aimed to instruct Dan himself, who, like Alwyn Tower in *The
Grandmothers,* serves not only as the repository and articulator of
their message, but becomes, in due course, their prime beneficiary.
Book one recounts the exemplum of Hannah Madoc, Dan's spiritual mother. Hannah is known as Bad Han, the local whore with
the golden heart; she is the jilted love of Dan's uncle and spiritual father, Jule Bier.

Because Jule is an obedient son, he accedes to his father's
wishes and renounces Hannah to marry the Puritanical Selma
Duncan, who is affluent, morally upright, and socially appropriate.
As a result, Hannah, whose family is not socially acceptable (her
father is a drunkard), becomes the handy sex object of all the
local bar aficionados. But Hannah has "gone to the bad" only ex-
ternally. Life's tests have strengthened her character and given
her inner peace. And Jule, whose love for and faith in Hannah
remain intact, despite his marriage *á la mode,* rescues her from
a bordello and returns her to her father's farm.

Once she is re-established on the land, she manages to work
out her own unique expiation. Indeed, Wescott portrays Hannah
almost as an Hawthornesque Hester Prynne, a totally self-reliant
woman, a nurse, a healer, a figure of valor and compassion for
whom the years pass in work and solitude. But even in old age
she remains an enigma to her small-town neighbors.

> As she grew old, she withdrew from the daily life of the
> people. Some hesitated to interrupt the curious preoccupation in
> which she visibly moved; others she repulsed sternly, saying "I
> have other work to do." Her strength was spent in obscure hurry-

ings, upon mysterious errands and appointments. The old woman was faithful to no tangible thing but her cow. In the common mind, she grew legendary, a mad old object of rags and dirt, a glance direct as an axe, a mop of iron-grey hair. Her figure agitated against the sunset in empty lanes, or proclaimed itself with an abrupt shout from a dark thicket or hollow. One met her on the roads, or found her in her garden: straw in her hair, an ethereal light in her eyes, a serene, incomprehensible smile on her square leather-coloured face.[4]

The Hindu overtones (her love of cattle), the pagan traits evident in her night journeys and her corn god-like attire of straw and rags (the scarecrow image is also obvious)—these are significant not only in themselves, but in the power and influence they assume for Dan. In sum, Hannah's life serves as a religious, ethical, and sexual touchstone for Dan. Her end is calm and Christlike. "She lay unconscious on her back, her face turned upward, her arms thrown out at her sides, her legs crumpled horribly under her heavy body. . . . Jule did everything for her. . . . Their eyes, when they did not run out over the marsh, were fixed upon each other; his gaze abstract, as if it gleaned then from her sunken, unlighted face her wisdom and her peace; the dying woman's wistful and proud, who entrusted her existence, from that moment, to his thought" (pp. 82, 86). Thus Hannah's story becomes a part of Jule's experience; Jule will tell it to his spiritual son, Dan, who, through the media of art (the book itself), imparts it to us.

But Hannah and Jule provide only one conduit that nourishes and influences Dan's quest for religious, ethical, and sexual individuation. In the second book, which deals more directly with Dan's coming of age, we meet Rosalia, the daughter of Selma and Jule Bier, Jule's hired man Michael Byron, who becomes Rosalia's lover, and Dan himself, Rosalia's cousin and Mike's friend. The book commences with the passing of grandfather Duncan, who represents the tradition of rigorous puritanism which is a charac-

4. Glenway Wescott, *The Apple of the Eye* (New York: Dial, 1924), p. 81. Subsequent references are to this edition, and page numbers of excerpts are given parenthetically in the text.

teristic of the Duncan and Strane families. The tone of the minister's eulogy makes the point: "The death of this good man is a warning. He has little to fear at the last day. . . . As for us, . . . we are wandering sheep, a spotted flock. . . . This is a day of corruption. Our young men are mere animals from whom every chaste woman should flee in terror, and our girls lead them on with indecent dresses and gestures. I tell you, my friends, the poison is in our flesh" (p. 99).

The bleak precepts of the Stranes and Duncans are juxtaposed against the dionysian, hedonistic desires of Mike Byron. At the edge of grandfather Duncan's grave, Mike, true to his poet namesake, decides not only to seduce Rosalia, but also to help Dan out of his jejune innocence. In the dialogue between Dan (innocence) and Mike (experience) interesting anti-puritanic arguments are posed.

> "Tell me then," he [Dan] asked, "don't you believe in chastity?"
>
> Mike's eyes brightened at an opportunity to teach. "What a queer question! It has beauty. Before I went to the university I thought it was the only thing. To live in the spirit instead of the flesh. . . . Then you feel that you're like Christ and all the saints. Puritanism appeals to the imagination, but it makes people sick. . . . You see, there isn't anything but flesh." He spoke slowly, in broken phrases, pronouncing the words with obvious pleasure. "We are all flesh; when it's weak, we're weak; when it's sick, we're sick; when it's dead, we're dead. Now we're civilized, we try to pretend that our bodies don't matter. But our minds, our imaginations, are flesh too, and part of the whole. . . . Your religion is wrong. . . . It cuts us in two." (pp. 133–34)

Significantly, Mike's precepts are clearly at variance with those of the Stranes. And these tensions cut Rosalia and Dan "in two," for Mike decides to move to a new job in another part of the country after initiating (some would say corrupting) Dan and Rosalia psychologically and sexually. Wescott nonetheless portrays Mike more sympathetically than the Stranes. The Rousseauesque Mike Byron does not physically reappear in the book, but Rosalia and Dan are left to grapple with the ideas he has infused in them. For Rosalia, who believes herself pregnant with Mike Byron's child, this encounter with alien precepts and extramarital sex proves fatal. She is driven to icy suicide in the bogs. She cannot handle her new sexual knowledge, nor can she deal with the emotional burden Mike has imparted to her. Dan, however, unlike Rosalia, *is* able successfully to sift these experiences and memories. Because he can do so, because he *can* reconcile himself to the antinomies, he has the opportunity to regain his physical and spiritual health. To that end, Dan, in book three, seeks the counsel of his uncle Jule.

In the last book, aptly titled "Dan Alone," the arduous religious, ethical, and sexual problems are resolved ultimately. Interestingly, the external landscape mirrors Dan's inner turmoil. The atmosphere is charged with jokes and bitterness, with juxtapositions of wonderland and wasteland, with fatigue and corruption, with fatal beauty. A storm occurs; then a rainbow appears. "These things met the boy's morose eyes. But there burned in them the faint fire of a determination to discover beauty; and he ignored them. The fantastic loveliness in his mind ceaselessly sought its counterpart in reality. His ideal love hunted its embodiment. The town was an arid hunting-ground" (p. 225).

Rosalia, whom Dan and Jule have recently buried in a secret forest grove, survives still in Dan's psyche. To retain his mental stability Rosalia's spirit must be propitiated; her death must be explained, absorbed, validated.

He hated Mike and all that he had meant, and determined to obliterate from his memory every trace of him. As he struggled with the images in his mind, and the long treasured words, and the echoes of emotion, they grew strong—deformed parts of himself, to be stifled, to be mutilated, to be killed. Mike's laughing philosophy, his exaltation of sensuality, his evil love of life, his poetry—their fruit was a little rotting body, bundled together in a horse-blanket. The dimmest recollection of Mike's appearance produced nausea, faintness, and the tingling of fear. Dan was pursued by the eyes, the mouth, the voice, the laughter, the freckled cheeks, the long arms, the brown fingers which had killed

Rosalia, and like a hunted animal fled from his own memory.
(pp. 252–53)

But memory ultimately becomes the healer as well as the
destroyer. In a dankly exotic, highly personal dark night of the
soul, Dan wrestles to exorcise the demons that possess him. Again
external landscape complements Dan's psychological state. "The
elaborate vegetation had a gross, charnel beauty. Under its actual
greens and yellows, the boy detected blackness. In spite of the
florid surface, it was a black land. A black land being consumed
by fire—slime-green tongues, and fetid smoke in the shape of
flowers" (p. 260).

Eventually the rank growths, the malevolent flowers, the
visions of the fire-blackened earthly morass subside. And his
uncle Jule administers to the boy's needs. It is Jule, his spiritual
father, who, by recounting Hannah's story (now charged with
universal meaning), effects Dan's individuation.

> When he [Jule] had finished Han stood, very strange and vivid,
> in the boy's mind. He might have known her, and forgotten, and
> remembered again. She looked like one who had never died, who
> never could be killed. Though Dan had seen her grave, he felt
> that she was not in it; surely the death of despair and dismay—
> the death he understood—had never brought her there. Then he
> realized that her life was like one of Mike's Greek myths.
>   The boy thought, How powerful a story is, and how by a
> kind of magic it compels the imagination; there was nothing in
> the world, it seemed to him, so mysteriously strong; and he began
> to wonder if he would ever have anything as beautiful to tell.
> (pp. 272–73)

Having gleaned the message of these tales and comprehended
how he now can deal with these events, Dan determines to leave
his home, to go to the university, to move out into the world.
"Now the ghosts which he imagined lingering along its [the
town's] thoroughfares, and the living ones he loved were at peace
and willing to let him go" (p. 291). At last Dan is prepared to re-
count his experience, which is in fact the book, a Faulknerian

amalgam of perceptions past and current, and to place his own mark on the story.

The book concludes with Dan confidently facing an outward journey, securely holding three chrysanthemums. They are the final detail of this maturation narrative; perhaps they symbolize harvest, cheer, optimism, rest, ease, long life, and happiness.[5] Perhaps they suggest the three divisions of the book, the three father figures (Jule Bier, John Strane, and Mike Byron), the three mother figures (Hannah Madoc, Theodora Strane, and Rosalia Bier), or the three problems which Dan must resolve (religious dogma, ethical choices, sexual awareness). Whatever the nature of the chrysanthemum symbolism, Wescott's ultimate tone infers that Dan has these matters well in hand as he begins another phase of his life's journey.

5. Ernst and Johanna Lehner, *Folklore and Symbolism of Flowers, Plants, and Trees* (New York: Tudor, 1960), p. 113.

Renaissance and Modern

was composed in 11-point Linotype Caledonia, leaded two points,
with display type handset in Libra by Joe Mann Associates;
printed offset on Hammermill 55-pound Lock Haven Offset
by Wickersham Printing Company;
Smyth-sewn and bound in Columbia Bayside Chambray over boards
by Vail-Ballou Press, Inc.;

published by SKIDMORE COLLEGE

and produced and distributed by

SYRACUSE UNIVERSITY PRESS

Syracuse, New York 13210